"[The book] is ideally suited to my class of young adults because of its logical organization, variety, and essential clarity." Quoted by permission.
—Shân Evans, English Department
John Abbott College
Ste. Anne de Bellevue, Québec

From a review [*TESL Communiqué* 2:1 (autumn 1977)] by Carol Fraser, Director of ESL Credit Courses at Concordia University in Montreal—

"For years... I have felt the need for a beginning adult composition text. In business or at school, our students need to write using a basic expository form; writing grammar exercises hasn't necessarily helped them to do this. *Composition Steps*, by the late Vivian Horn, goes a long way towards answering this need.... *Composition Steps* does not assume that students using it can already write correct sentences.... The nicest thing about [the book] is the wide variety of exercises for students.... This text certainly exemplifies the belief that students learn by doing...." Quoted by permission.

Composition Steps

Composition Steps

Vivian Horn
edited and annotated by Esther Rosman

NEWBURY HOUSE PUBLISHERS, Cambridge
A division of Harper & Row, Publishers, Inc.
New York, Philadelphia, San Francisco, Washington
London, Mexico City, São Paulo, Singapore, Sydney

Library of Congress Cataloging in Publication Data

Horn, Vivian.
   Composition steps.

   1. English language--Paragraphs. 2. English
language--Rhetoric. I. Rosman, Esther.
II. Title.
PE1439.H57   808'.042   76-57147
ISBN 0-88377-069-5

Cover design by Michael Giaquinto

NEWBURY HOUSE PUBLISHERS
A division of Harper & Row, Publishers, Inc.

 Language Science
Language Teaching
Language Learning

CAMBRIDGE, MASSACHUSETTS

Copyright © 1977 by Newbury House Publishers, Inc. All rights reserved. No part of this book may be reproduced or transmitted in any form or by any means, electronic or mechanical, including photocopying, recording, or by any information storage and retrieval system, without permission in writing from the Publisher.

Printed in the U.S.A.   First printing: April 1977

CONTENTS

Introduction to the Teacher		1
Introduction to the Student (What this book is about)		5
Unit 1	**Types of Writing:** Narration—time order; Description—space order; Exposition—logical order *Skills: Free composition for evaluation*	6
Unit 2	**Exposition—logical order:** Unity—one topic; Irrelevant sentences *Skills: Capital letters; Periods; Spelling*	12
Unit 3	**Finding the topic:** One topic in a paragraph; The topic sentence; Topic and statement *Skills: Structure exercises—Changing questions to statements; Spelling; Syllabification*	18
Unit 4	Review—Writing topic sentences. Adding details. "List" paragraphs. Kinds of details *Skills: Copyreading; Distinguishing fact from opinion; Punctuation; Spelling; Vocabulary; Word game*	25
Unit 5	Supporting sentences for the topic sentence. Logical order of sentences in a paragraph. Coherence *Skills: Punctuation; Structure exercise; Recognizing complete and incomplete sentences; Spelling*	34
Unit 6	Coherence of a paragraph. **Links between sentences:** Repetition of key words; Pronouns. Review—Irrelevant sentences *Skills: Punctuation; Spelling*	43
Unit 7	**Choosing topic sentences:** Paragraphs without a topic sentence. Review—kinds of paragraphs. Relevance—choosing sentences that support the topic sentence *Skills: Punctuation; Capital Letters; Commas and periods; Spelling; Vocabulary game; Syllabification*	49
Unit 8	**Completeness of paragraphs:** Recognizing when paragraphs are incomplete. Sentence links—possessive adjectives. Writing a paragraph in answer to questions *Skills: Subject and object pronouns; Possessive adjectives; Grammar exercise; Complete and incomplete sentences; Spelling*	55

Contents

Unit 9	Review—sentence links. Using *this, that, these, those* with a noun. Choosing relevant sentences to support a paragraph *Skills: Finding mistakes in grammar; Structure exercise; Spelling*	**64**
Unit 10	Review. Choosing topic sentences. Finding irrelevant sentences. Logical order of sentences. Changing questions to statements. *Skills: Copyreading—finding mistakes in capitalization and grammar; Recognizing nouns, verbs, adjectives and adverbs; Personal pronouns and possessive adjectives; Spelling review; Free composition for comparison with Unit 1*	**69**
Unit 11	**Letter writing—personal and business letters:** Form for a business letter; Appearance of a letter. Sentence links—review; New Link—*this that, these, those* without a noun. Answering questions to form a paragraph *Skills: Irregular verbs; Spelling*	**75**
Unit 12	Dependent sentences—signals that point to a preceding sentence or sentences. **Letter writing—addressing the envelope:** Folding a letter *Skills: Structure Exercise—using nouns, verbs, adjectives and adverbs; Agreement of subject and verb; Capitalization and grammar; Recognizing complete and incomplete sentences; Spelling; Alphabetical order*	**85**
Unit 13	Identifying paragraphs that have topic sentences. Coherence—arranging "scrambled" paragraphs in correct order. Paragraph completion—using relevant sentences *Skills: Structure exercise—writing sentences using but; Spelling; Vocabulary; Distinguishing between their and there*	**94**
Unit 14	**Choosing supporting details:** Writing main points of supporting sentences. Writing topic sentences for supporting details. Review—letter writing. Writing a paragraph by answering questions *Skills: Copyreading—correcting errors in spelling and grammar; Abbreviations; Complete and incomplete sentences; Writing sentences using but; Alphabetical order; Spelling; Vocabulary*	**101**
Unit 15	**Identifying topics:** Choosing sentences that belong to topic A or B. Identifying main supporting details *Skills: Structure exercise; Review—irregular verbs; Position of adverbs; Copyreading; Spelling review; Vocabulary game*	**111**
Unit 16	Developing the topic. Review—additional details—using examples—signals of examples, Writing examples. Rewriting "scrambled" paragraphs. Writing topic sentences *Skills: Punctuation—commas; Alphabetical order; Using two, to and too; Spelling—ing form of verbs; Vocabulary*	**118**

Contents

Unit 17	Review—using examples to develop a topic. Writing paragraphs using examples. Choosing relevant sentences and arranging them in logical order *Skills: Copyreading—errors in capitalization and grammar; Spelling; Vocabulary game*	127
Unit 18	"Dicto-Comp" exercise. Sentence link review. New sentence link—synonyms. Review—relevance and coherence. Writing a paragraph using examples *Skills: Structure exercise—ing form; Spelling; Vocabulary*	132
Unit 19	Developing the topic. Review—using examples. Giving reasons—identifying topics that require reasons. Recognizing paragraphs developed by using reasons. Review—letter writing *Skills: Copyreading—periods and capital letters; Syllabification; Alphabetical order; Spelling; Vocabulary*	139
Unit 20	Identifying paragraphs that use reasons. Writing a free paragraph using reasons. Analyzing a paragraph. Final review *Skills: Copyreading—punctuation, capitalization, forms of nouns, verbs and pronouns; Following directions*	145

Composition Steps

INTRODUCTION TO THE TEACHER

The purpose of this book is to introduce students to the principles of expository writing. Because the book is intended for adults with a limited educational background, its approach is simple but not juvenile.

1. *Exposition.* The emphasis is on expository writing because this is the kind that students need most, in school and on a job. It is also the kind of writing in which organization is most necessary and most difficult. Since it calls for a logical approach, students must be guided in certain ways of thinking.

At the start there is a brief discussion of narration and description only to try to make clearer what exposition is. It is likely that students will not immediately understand exposition, but it is hoped that they will gradually get a feeling for it as they proceed through the lessons. They will also gain understanding of terms like *logical order, relevance, coherence,* etc. Although the terms are defined, their real meaning will probably sink in only gradually. The use of such terms is kept to a minimum, but a few are considered necessary.

2. *Paragraph structure.* Many composition books deal mainly with sentence structure. They introduce students to paragraph structure at the end and leave them at that point. This book starts out with paragraph structure and emphasizes it throughout. It does not assume, however, that students are able to write entirely correct sentences; it assumes that they will practice writing sentences and paragraphs concurrently, under the teacher's direction. It is felt that *composition* involves the arrangement of sentences in larger units than the sentence and that if this arrangement must wait until students perfect their control of the sentence, it may never begin. The principal aim here is to develop a sense of structure and organization.

3. *Learning by Doing.* For students who have little or no experience with writing, it does no good to admonish them to "write clearly" or to "stick to the point." They need to have the meaning of such terms demonstrated in some way and then to have ample opportunity for practice. The emphasis here is on *doing* and explanations are kept brief. Where explanation is presented, the teacher should read through the explanation with the students; first, because students are often reluctant to read such explanations on their own, and second, because they may not understand them—particularly in the first stages of the lessons—if they do read them on their own. However, the reading and comprehension of such explanations is part of their training.

4. *Sequence.* The lessons are sequenced in small, clear-cut steps, one point at a time, with activities for practicing each step. Frequently the first activity is a recognition or identification exercise as preparation for a doing exercise. The first examples are intended to be easy and obvious.

Introduction to the Teacher

5. *Controlled Writing.* The progression is from controlled to semi-free and free writing. However, even in early stages occasional free writing is provided, both for a change of pace and to give students a chance to try their wings. It also gives the teacher a chance to appraise the degree of progress.

6. *Variety of Activities.* Aside from following the principle of slowly decreasing controls, no specific approach is taken. In the belief that there is no one best way of developing writing ability, a large variety of exercises is used. Writing is difficult and calls for many skills. Students differ widely. At this stage of our knowledge, no one can say with certainty which activities are most effective. Hence, we believe that the more varied the exercises, the better.

Another reason for variety: it is possible that the students aimed at may require more than the usual amount of variety to keep up interest.

Following is a list of the types of activities used. It is not complete because it does not show all the variations of some activities nor combinations of activities.

Copying	Forming paragraphs by answering questions
Identification/recognition	Imitating model paragraphs
Dictation	Punctuation
"Scrambled" paragraphs	Copyreading
Grammar	Word games
Spelling	Following directions
Alphabetizing	Letter writing
Oral composition	Dicto-comps
Paragraph completion	Free writing

7. *Grammar.* Grammar exercises are provided in many units, but they are not intended as a course in grammar. As already pointed out, the focus is on paragraph writing rather than on sentence writing. We assume that students have had some grammar and may be concurrently studying grammar. The grammar exercises are intentionally very elementary and are meant to serve only as a refresher and reminder, by way of preparing the students for certain types of composition exercises. The responsibility for additional work on sentence construction is left to the teacher. The book does not endeavor to *teach* grammar as such.

8. *Spelling.* Spelling exercises are provided in most of the units. They do not comprise a thorough or carefully structured course in spelling, but rather are a means of keeping students constantly aware of spelling. The words included in spelling lists are taken mainly from lists of frequently misspelled words, although some words are included to provide examples for spelling rules.

The spelling words are not presented in context; that is, example sentences are not given. It is therefore the teacher's responsibility to provide appropriate sentences. We felt that the teacher will be better able to furnish sentences that tie in closely with the classroom situation.

9. *Vocabulary.* As with grammar, the book does not strive to *teach* vocabulary as such, although it will undoubtedly stimulate the learning of a certain amount of new vocabulary.

Introduction to the Teacher

While an effort has been made to keep the example and practice paragraphs simple, vocabulary is not strictly controlled. There is no way of knowing what kind of controls would be practical, since we assume that the book will be used in a wide variety of classes. Most students will have a very limited vocabulary in some areas and a sophisticated vocabulary in others.

Although the vocabulary has been kept fairly simple, we believe that occasional instances of unusual or difficult words do no harm; in fact, some students seem to enjoy them. Such words, when they occur, are used mainly for recognition, not for production.

We assume that students can read on a higher level than that on which they can write. Consequently, paragraphs for identification and for copying are more difficult than any the students are expected to produce themselves.

10. *Subject Matter.* Example and practice paragraphs intentionally cover a wide range of subjects. Some are related to the probable immediate environment of the students and some are entirely apart from it. We believe that both kinds have value, and it is difficult to predict what will be of most interest.

11. *Repetition.* There is some repetition in the subject matter of paragraphs; that is, occasionally a paragraph may be similar to a previous paragraph used for another purpose. We believe that students sometimes welcome subject matter that is familiar or partly familiar, and of course repetition provides review.

12. *Copying.* In the course of rearranging scrambled paragraphs and similar exercises, students are asked to do a considerable amount of copying. We feel that this practice will improve the student's facility in writing and will also reinforce spelling, vocabulary, and sentence structure.

13. *Copyreading.* Beginning with early units, a good deal of emphasis is placed on copyreading practice. We believe that most composition books give too little practice of this kind. Students must somehow be trained to notice their own errors; they very often simply do not *see* errors. This ability can usually be developed with practice. Also, many students dislike checking their papers before handing them in; the aim here is to get them in the habit of doing this.

The first copyreading exercises have only one or two kinds of errors, and the students are told what to look for. The variety and number of errors are gradually increased.

14. *Sentence Links.* Considerable emphasis has been placed on links between sentences, in the belief that this is another area which is not usually given sufficient attention. As soon as students begin putting sentences together in paragraphs, they must become aware of a new set of relationships—those between sentences. The matter of inter-sentence connections is vitally important in learning to construct paragraphs, and it needs to be *taught*.

15. *Dictation, Paragraph Completion, Dicto-comps.* These activities are meant to provide listening practice as well as practice in grammar, spelling, punctuation, and other skills. The paragraph completion exercises are intended to serve as a link between dictation and dicto-comps.

16. *Teacher's Handbook.* A teacher's handbook is provided to make detailed suggestions for handling the material. For example, the unit that introduces business letter writing is very detailed, pointing out every small

Introduction to the Teacher

mechanical point. Students probably would not wade through this themselves. The teacher should go through this step-by-step with the students, illustrating each point on the board. After this careful procedure, the unit will serve as a place of reference for checking on details as the students do letter writing exercises in succeeding units.

INTRODUCTION TO THE STUDENT

WHAT THIS BOOK IS ABOUT

A. Many people find it easy to speak but hard to write things down on paper. It is important for many people, however, to know how to put things down on paper. It is important for those who want to go farther in school, for school work demands writing, and it is important for those who want better jobs. Good jobs in business go to those people who know how to express themselves well in *both* speaking and writing.

The purpose of this book is to teach some basic points about writing and to teach the writing of paragraphs. Paragraphs consist of sentences put together in certain ways. You probably know a lot about writing sentences already, and you will receive more practice writing sentences as you practice writing paragraphs. Paragraphs are like building blocks; you use them to build larger pieces of writing. When you finish this book you will know how to write basic kinds of paragraphs that will be useful for various purposes.

Writing is not easy. It involves much work and practice. Trying to put your ideas on paper in just the way you want them is never easy. When you write you have to think of several things at the same time. Some of them are:

Ideas	Grammar
Vocabulary	Punctuation
Spelling	Handwriting

You have to think of all these things even in a very simple piece of writing. And when you begin to write paragraphs, you have to think of additional points. This book will provide the practice you need and will illustrate the things you have to know.

There are various kinds of writing. This book deals mostly with just one kind, the kind of writing that is most useful for school and business. However, you need to know a little about the other kinds of writing, too.

UNIT 1

TYPES OF WRITING

B. Different types of writing are required for different purposes. In general, we can divide writing into three kinds: *narration, description,* and *exposition.*

Narration tells "what happened." It tells a story. It is the kind of writing that you find in novels, short stories, and biographies.

Description tells how something looks or feels or sounds. It talks about such features as size, shape, color, sound, or taste.

Exposition is writing that explains something. It often answers the questions *what, how,* and *why.* Its purpose is to present ideas and to make the ideas as clear as possible.

EXERCISE

C. Which of the three kinds of writing is illustrated by this paragraph?

One day a crow stole a piece of cheese from a woman's kitchen and flew with it to a tree. A fox who was very hungry saw the crow. He said to the crow, "You have a beautiful voice. Won't you sing for me?" The crow was very pleased by the compliment. As he opened his mouth to sing, the piece of cheese fell to the ground. The fox snatched the cheese and ran away.

Narration

Time Order

D. There are various ways to organize the sentences in a piece of writing. In narration the sentences are usually organized according to *time order.* One thing happens and then another thing happens, and the events are told in the same order.

You are familiar with time order because you have noticed it when you were reading stories. The story you just read about the fox and the crow follows time order. The sentences in the paragraph tell the story just as the events happened. To show the order of events, the sentences could be arranged like this:

1. A crow stole a piece of cheese from a woman's kitchen.
2. He flew with it to a tree.
3. A hungry fox saw the crow.
4. He said to the crow, "You have a beautiful voice. Won't you sing for me?"
5. The crow was very pleased by the compliment.
6. He opened his mouth to sing.
7. The piece of cheese fell to the ground.
8. The fox snatched the cheese.
9. He ran away.

Because the events happened in a certain order, it is important that the sentences in the story follow one another in a certain order. Suppose the sentences were arranged like this:

He ran away.
A crow stole a piece of cheese from a woman's kitchen.
A hungry fox saw the crow.
He opened his mouth to sing.
He said to the crow, "You have a beautiful voice. Won't you sing for me?"
etc.

If the sentences were arranged like this, the story would be so mixed up that you could not understand it. You can see how important it is to arrange the sentences in good order.

E. The sentences that follow have no order. Write the correct order on the lines provided.

EXERCISE

Example
1. *He looked especially at bicycles, radios, and phonograph records.*
2. *At four o'clock he went home.*
3. *He looked at various things.*
4. *John went to the shopping center yesterday.*

Correct order
__4__ , __3__ , __1__ , __2__

1. 1. George liked one of them.
    2. The librarian gave him three books to look at.
    3. George visited the library.
    4. He checked the book out and took it home with him.
    5. He asked for a book to read.   ____, ____, ____, ____, ____

2. 1. The small car turned over.
    2. There was an accident at the street corner.
    3. The two men inside it were badly injured.
    4. A large truck hit a small car.
    5. The police took them to a hospital.   ____, ____, ____, ____, ____

UNIT 1

3.
1. The house began to leak.
2. Then leaks began in other rooms.
3. Fortunately the rain stopped then and the sun came out.
4. The first leak started in the living room.
5. It rained steadily for two days.   ____, ____, ____, ____, ____

4.
1. They came to school ready to write the exam.
2. The students studied very hard for it.
3. He was sick that day.
4. They found that the teacher was not there.
5. The teacher said he would give an examination.   ____, ____, ____, ____, ____

5.
1. Two women were there.
2. Then the other had her hair washed and set.
3. Mary went to the beauty shop.
4. Finally the hairdresser was ready for Mary.
5. One woman had her hair cut.   ____, ____, ____, ____, ____

F. Think about the list of topics that follows. Put an X before each topic that you would probably develop according to time order if you were writing about it.

1. _____ The Importance of Good Health Habits
2. _____ My Vacation Trip
3. _____ Spring Is My Favorite Season
4. _____ The Characteristics of Indian Music
5. _____ Why I Want to Be a Lawyer
6. _____ How I Spent Last Sunday
7. _____ The Growth of Opportunities for Women in Business and the Professions
8. _____ My Favorite Actor

G. If the sentences in the example under exercise E were copied in paragraph form, they would look like this:

Assignment

    John went to the shopping center yesterday. He looked at various things. He looked especially at bicycles, radios, and phonograph records. At four o'clock he went home.

    In the same way, copy the sentences in exercise E in paragraph form. Write two paragraphs; you need not do all of them. Choose the two you wish to do. Write the sentences neatly in the same order in which you numbered them. Be sure to *indent* the first line in each paragraph.
    Number the sentences in the remaining three paragraphs in the order in which they should be copied.
    After you have copied the sentences in your two paragraphs, read the paragraphs to make sure that you have put the sentences in the correct time order. Also be sure that you have copied the sentences correctly, with no mistakes in spelling or punctuation.

UNIT 1

Description

H. You have seen that narration usually follows time order. *Description* may follow various kinds of order, depending on what is being described. If you are describing a man, you will choose different things to say than if you are describing a mountain or a restaurant or a dress.

Space Order

One kind of description follows *space order.* In space order you tell *where* things are. This is the order you will probably follow if you want to describe a place.

For example, here is a description of a classroom:

Example 1.   *The classroom is large, clean and well lighted. The walls are pale green. On the wall at the left as you enter there are three large windows. The teacher's desk is in the front. Blackboards cover most of the wall at the right.*

Notice that this writer describes how the room looks from the door—what is on the left, what is in front, and what is on the right. It does not matter which way you move in your description. The important thing is to have some order that will be easy for the reader to follow.

Now compare the description using space order with this description of a man:

Example 2.   *The man who opened the door in answer to my knock was an elderly man, white-haired and bent. He looked at me over his spectacles, which were far down on his nose. In spite of his age, his dark eyes were keen and his voice was clear and strong. I noticed that he was wearing a bright-colored sports shirt.*

In describing the man, the writer selected the man's most interesting and most outstanding features. This description is quite different from a description of a place based on space order. The kind of description you use depends on what you are describing.

Exposition

Logical Order

I. Narration tells what happened. Description tells how something looked or felt or sounded. *Exposition* explains something. Here are some examples of exposition:

Example 1.   *Our teeth are very important to us. There are two main uses for teeth. One is to chew our food, which then is easy to swallow and digest. The second use is to help us talk. We put our tongues against our teeth to make certain sounds. It is difficult to understand what a person is saying if he does not have any teeth.*

UNIT 1

Notice that this paragraph does not tell about a happening and it does not describe the teeth. The paragraph *explains* why our teeth are important.

Example 2. *The common housefly is very dangerous. It carries germs in its mouth and on its legs and feet. The legs and feet are covered with small hairs. On these hairs there are thousands and thousands of germs. One fly may carry as many as 6,000,000 germs. When a fly stops and eats some food, it leaves thousands of germs on the food.*

Notice that the first sentence says that the housefly is dangerous. Then the sentences that follow explain what this means. They explain by telling *why* the housefly is dangerous and *how* it spreads germs.

What kind of order does exposition follow? Because exposition tries to make ideas clear and understandable to the reader, we say that it follows *logical order*. There are various kinds of logical order. You will learn more about them as you go on in these composition lessons.

EXERCISE

J. See if you can identify the types of writing in the following paragraphs. Mark each paragraph N (for Narration), D (for Description), or E (for Exposition).

_____ 1. The robin is a common American bird. It grows about 9 or 10 inches long. The male has a rusty-red breast, dark gray upper parts, and a blackish head. Its tail feathers are tipped with white. The female is usually slightly smaller than the male and of duller color. Robins live in North America from Mexico to Alaska.

_____ 2. Special schools have been developed in Iran to meet the educational needs of nomads. Nomads are people who move from place to place. Because they move so often, their children cannot read or write. Consequently the government of Iran cannot send letters to them or make agreements with them. To solve the educational problem, the government has started schools in tents in the nomad camps.

_____ 3. The traveler stepped into the hall of the old castle and looked around. It was a large room with stone walls. Several sleeping dogs lay against the wall on the left. In the middle of the room there was a fire. The smoke rose to a hole in the ceiling, but some of it remained in the room. The windows, high in the wall on the right, were not very large and the great room was rather dark.

_____ 4. In 1928 an English doctor was working in his laboratory in a London hospital. The doctor's name was Alexander Fleming. One day he found a tiny bit of mold in a dish that he was using in his work. He started to throw the mold away. Then he noticed that it seemed unusual. He kept the mold and studied it for a long time. He discovered that it could kill germs. He named it *penicillin*.

_____ 5. Many foods contain small amounts of substances called vitamins. Vitamins are necessary to the health of the body. Even if we eat a lot of food, we will not be healthy unless the food contains enough vitamins. Vitamins are important for healthy eyes and skin, strong bones and teeth, normal growth, and the regulation of the work of the body's organs.

Mixed Writing

It is not always easy to decide what is narration, what is description, and what is exposition. Often a piece of writing includes all three types. A narration may include some description and some exposition. An exposition may use some narration and description in order to explain something as completely as possible. Usually it is possible, however, to decide whether a piece of writing is *mainly* narration or *mainly* description or *mainly* exposition.

Assignment

1. In this assignment you will practice using time order. You are to write a paragraph on the subject: "What I Did Yesterday." Begin with what you did in the morning and go through the day, following time order. Since you are telling what has already happened, remember to use the past tense of verbs—for example, *worked, walked, ate, did*.

Also remember to *indent* the first line of your paragraph. When you finish your composition, read it carefully and correct any mistakes you have made in capitalization, punctuation, or spelling. Remember that you start every sentence with a capital letter and end most sentences with a period.

Dictation

2. Study the story about the fox and the crow (page 6) carefully. Notice the punctuation. Learn the spelling of any words that are new to you. Be prepared to write this paragraph from dictation.

UNIT 2

Dictation

A. Do the dictation exercise that was assigned in the preceding unit.

EMPHASIS ON EXPOSITION

B. Although you need to practice the three types of writing, most of the work in this course will be on exposition. This is the type of writing that is most needed by students. After you finish school, you will also need to use this kind of writing more than another kind.

Most of your reading will also be the expository type, for that is the type found in textbooks, newspaper and magazine articles, essays, reports, and nonfiction in general. Of course you may also read literature—novels, short stories, drama, and poetry—but most of your reading will be of expository material.

Because the emphasis here will be on exposition, most of the paragraphs you will discuss and write will be paragraphs of exposition. Expository paragraphs have certain types of organization that need to be learned.

Logical Order

C. Narration usually follows time order and description sometimes follows space order. We say that exposition follows logical order. This means that the paragraphs are arranged in such a way that the reader can understand the writer's thinking.

In time order the writer guides the reader from one happening to another. In space order the writer guides the reader from one place to another. In logical order the writer guides the reader from one *idea* to another.

One Topic

D. One part of logical order is that all the sentences in a paragraph refer to the same topic. Look at these sentences:

Example 1. *The sky is very blue today. He lives in a large house. Elephants are large animals. Many foods contain small amounts of substances called vitamins. I like ice cream.*

What is this paragraph about? It is impossible to say what it is about. Is it really a paragraph? It looks like one because the first sentence is indented. But it is not a paragraph. It has no single topic. Each sentence is about something different. The sentences have no relation to each other. They do not make sense.

Now look at these sentences:

Example 2.   *There is a book on the desk. It is a large book. It is new. It is a chemistry book.*

What is this paragraph about? It is easy to see that it is about a book. These are very simple sentences. Is it possible for such simple sentences to form a paragraph? Yes, because they all deal with a single topic. All the sentences refer to a certain book. That means that all the sentences are about the same topic.

UNITY

E. When all the sentences in a paragraph are about the same topic, the paragraph forms a unit. We say the paragraph has *unity*. Unity helps the reader to follow the writer's thought. A paragraph has unity when every sentence sticks to the subject.

EXERCISE

F. Read these paragraphs and decide what each one is about. Does each sentence deal only with a single topic?

1. Bicycles provide a simple form of transportation. They are used for both pleasure and business. The word *bicycle* means "two wheels." The rider pedals with his feet to make the wheels move. No one knows who built the first bicycle.

2. Thomas A. Edison was an American inventor. He was born in Ohio in 1847. Throughout his life he worked in various technical and scientific fields. He became very successful and famous. Perhaps his most important invention was the electric light.

What is the topic of paragraph 1? What is the topic of paragraph 2?
Now read the next paragraph and notice its topic. Does every sentence deal with the topic?

3. Scientists have made a new type of rubber. This type of rubber has certain advantages over the older types. Plastic materials also have many advantages. So far this type of rubber is produced only in the laboratory, but later it may be made in factories.

The topic of this paragraph is a new type of rubber. However, the third sentence mentions plastic materials, which have no relation to the topic. Therefore, this sentence does not belong in the paragraph.

UNIT 2

The next two paragraphs also contain sentences that are not directly related to the topic. Underline these unrelated sentences.

4. I never know what to do with my hands when I am giving a talk. For instance, when I am making an oral report in history class, I have trouble with my hands. Sometimes I put them behind me. At other times I hide them in my pockets. A good speaker does not pause very much while he is speaking. Often I clasp my hands in front of me to keep them from shaking while I am speaking.

5. It was really a perfect day. It was a day that made everything seem beautiful. The sun shone brightly, but it was not too hot. The flowers seemed to open up wider in the lovely weather. It was a day when the world seemed brighter and happier than usual. In the winter I have to stay indoors so much that I like to be outdoors in the summer.

Irrelevant Sentences

G. If a sentence does not deal with the topic of the paragraph, we say that it is *irrelevant*. This means that it is not closely related to the other sentences in the paragraph. If a sentence is irrelevant, it does not belong in the paragraph and should be taken out. If a paragraph contains irrelevant material, it does not have unity.

H. Here are more paragraphs that contain irrelevant material. Underline the sentences that you consider irrelevant.

EXERCISE

1. Diamonds are the most valuable of the precious stones. They were first discovered in India, probably around 500 B.C. For a long time India was the only source of diamonds. Later large diamond fields were discovered in Africa. Many rubies and other precious stones come from Burma. The largest and most perfect diamonds are so valuable that they are priceless. Most of these stones are now held by museums and governments.

2. Many of the vegetables we buy when we go to the supermarket are "naturalized Americans." Originally they came from faraway places. Tomatoes and the so-called Irish potatoes came from South America. Cucumbers and eggplant originated in India. Radishes came from China. No one knows where apples and pears were first found, but scientists believe peaches came from China. Peas, carrots, lettuce, and parsnips are also from Asia.

3. Japan consists of a group of four large islands and hundreds of small ones. The largest and most important island is Honshu, on which the six chief cities are situated. The island of Shikoku, south of Honshu, is one of the chief rice-growing regions. Kyushu is the most southerly of the large islands. North of Honshu is Hokkaido, which is more thinly populated than the other large islands. Spring and summer are usually very pleasant.

4. Ice cream is so common in our lives that we never think about how we came to have it. Who first made ice cream? It is thought that ice cream, like many other things, originated in China. Some other inventions by the Chinese are said to be gunpowder, paper, and silk cloth. It is believed that a traveler brought the idea from China to Italy several centuries ago. From Italy it spread to France and England, and later to the United States.

5. The idea behind credit cards is that someone trusts us and believes that we will pay for something at a later date. The use of credit in business is very old. People have given other people credit for thousands of years in many different parts of the world. The modern credit card, however, has been in use only since about 1950. Many changes in business have taken place in recent years. Now people use credit cards for food, lodging, goods and services of all kinds.

Assignment

I. Each of the following paragraphs includes irrelevant material. Read the paragraphs and cross out the sentences you consider irrelevant. Then copy the paragraphs, omitting the irrelevant material. Be sure that you copy the other sentences correctly and that you indent the first line of each paragraph.

1. Today we depend on electricity more than we realize. Electricity gives us light in darkness, warmth in winter, and coolness in summer. It cooks our food and washes our clothes and dishes. It helps us shave, sew, and clean the house. Electricity gives us movies and television to entertain us in our free time. Sometimes storms cut off the supply of electricity.

2. Most ants are hard workers. They often work from six o'clock in the morning until ten o'clock at night. Ants may live to be a year old, and some have been known to live six or seven years. The work is divided among the ants so that each one has a certain amount to do. We do not know how they decide what work each one is to do.

3. Dr. Alexander Fleming was studying bacteria. In his laboratory he was growing a certain kind of harmful bacteria in small dishes. One morning he came to work as usual. It was a beautiful fall morning. He looked at his dishes of bacteria and noticed something unusual. In one dish there was a greenish-blue mold.

Reminder: Capital Letters and Periods

Now, before you hand in your papers, check them to make sure that you have started every sentence with a capital letter and ended it with a period. Periods are very small but important.

UNIT 2

Capital Letters

J. In addition to capitalizing the first word in a sentence, you should also capitalize these kinds of words:

1. Names of persons (*Tom Brown, Sue Sweet*)
2. Names of countries, states, and cities (*Italy, Minnesota, Dallas*)
3. Names of the days of the week (*Monday, Tuesday*)
4. Names of the months of the year (*January, February*)

EXERCISE

K. Rewrite these sentences, putting in capital letters.

1. john myers, a member of the los angeles quartet, lives on sunset boulevard.

2. the white house in washington is the official residence of the president of the united states.

3. mr. and mrs. james harrigan always visit ireland in june and scotland in september.

4. last monday gordon childers forgot to set his alarm and missed his plane to rome, italy.

5. in january and february the weather is so severe in new england that alice and thomas roberts go to miami, florida.

Spelling

L. Here are some words that were used in this unit and in Unit 1. You should learn the spelling of these words. Of course you should also know the meaning and pronunciation of each word.

Nouns

NOTICE THE DOUBLE LETTERS
a<u>cc</u>ident — a<u>cc</u>idents
ho<u>sp</u>ital — hospitals
information — *no plural*

NOTICE THE FIRST r.
lib<u>r</u>ary — lib<u>r</u>aries

Adjectives
important
beautiful

UNIT 2

Verbs
explain — explains — explained
describe — describes — described
notice — notices — noticed

Adverb
us<u>u</u>a<u>ll</u>y

NOTICE THE <u>u</u> AFTER <u>s</u> AND
THE DOUBLE LETTERS.

Assignment

M. Study the following paragraph. Notice the punctuation. Be sure you know the spelling of all the words. Be prepared to write this paragraph from dictation.

Dictation. There was an accident at the street corner. A large truck hit a small car. The small car turned over. The two men inside it were badly injured. They were taken to a hospital. The police asked for information about the accident. The truck driver explained that his brakes did not hold.

UNIT 3

Dictation

A. Do the dictation that was assigned in the previous unit.

FINDING THE TOPIC

B. You have seen that in a good paragraph all the sentences deal with one topic. It is important to recognize the topic. Look at this paragraph:

Example 1. *Shopping is hard for me. I get very tired walking around in large department stores. Having to choose among several items is often confusing. Even though there is so much merchandise very often I can't find what I am looking for. For example, if I am looking for a blouse, they may have the color I want, but not in my size. If the blouse is the right size, it is the wrong color.*

What is the topic of this paragraph? Check one.
_____ a. shopping
_____ b. large department stores
_____ c. wrong merchandise

The paragraph says something about large department stores and about wrong merchandise, but that is only part of the paragraph. The whole paragraph is about shopping. The topic of this paragraph is *shopping.*

Now read this paragraph:

Example 2. *Shopping on Saturday is usually tiresome. The stores are crowded. Too many people are doing their shopping on the same day. They all want to be waited on at the same time. Usually service is slow because there are not enough clerks to take care of the extra people. Often both the clerks and the customers become irritable.*

What is the topic of this paragraph? Check one.
_____ a. shopping
_____ b. crowds in the stores
_____ c. shopping on Saturday

Does this paragraph have the same topic as paragraph 1? If it is different, how is it different?

Here is another paragraph:

Example 3. *Getting to school in winter is difficult. Getting up in the morning is always hard, but getting up while it is still dark makes it more difficult. It is unpleasant to go out into the cold, dark morning. It is even more unpleasant to stand on the corner and shiver while waiting for the bus.*

What is the topic of this paragraph? Check one.
_____ a. getting up in winter
_____ b. getting to school
_____ c. getting to school in winter

THE TOPIC SENTENCE

C. You have probably noticed that in the paragraphs you have read, the topic is given in the first sentence. This sentence tells you immediately what the paragraph is about and what you can expect to find in the paragraph. The sentence that gives you the topic of the paragraph is called *the topic sentence.*

When the topic sentence opens the paragraph, it makes a general statement about a subject. The other sentences in the paragraph give more details to complete the picture.

You saw that there was a difference between paragraph 1 and paragraph 2. Paragraph 1 was about shopping in general, but paragraph 2 was about a certain kind of shopping—shopping on Saturday. What do you notice about paragraph 3? You see that it is not about getting to school, but about getting to school at a certain time—in winter.

It is important to know the correct topic of a paragraph.

Topic and Statement

D. 1. Here are the topic sentences for the example paragraphs in this unit:

a. Shopping is hard for me.
b. Shopping on Saturday is usually tiresome.
c. Getting to school in winter is difficult.

If you look at these sentences carefully, you will see that each sentence has two parts; the subject, which names what is being talked about, and the predicate, which completes the general statement about the subject. For ease of discussion, the topic sentence can be broken down into "topic" and "statement about the topic."

	Topic	*Statement about the topic*
Sentence a.	shopping	is difficult for me
Sentence b.	shopping on Saturday	is usually tiresome

Fill in the blanks for topic sentence c:

Sentence c. _____   _____

UNIT 3

2. Here are some topic sentences from paragraphs you have read in the preceding units. For each sentence, give the topic and then give the statement that is made about the topic.

EXERCISE

a. Our teeth are very important to us.
b. The common housefly is very dangerous.
c. Bicycles provide a simple form of transportation.
d. Thomas A. Edison was an American inventor.
e. Diamonds are the most valuable of the precious stones.

Writing Topic Sentences

E. Read the following sentences. This is not a good paragraph, but it is being used to illustrate a point. Is there a topic sentence in this paragraph?

1. May was hot. June was hot. July was hot. August was hot. September was hot.

   Which of the items below is the best topic?
   a. July weather
   b. weather
   c. the weather last spring and summer

   Which of the words below best expresses what should be said about the topic?
   a. unusual
   b. hot
   c. rainy

Now you know the topic of the paragraph and what should be said about the topic. On the blank line write a suitable topic sentence for the paragraph (E.1).

_____

Here is another group of sentences:

2. The news was bad on Monday. The news was bad on Tuesday. The news was bad on Wednesday. The news was bad on Thursday and Friday.

20

UNIT 3

Which of the items below is the best topic?
a. the news
b. bad news
c. the news last week

Which of the words below best expresses what should be said about the topic?
a. important
b. bad
c. cheerful

Now you know the topic of the paragraph and what should be said about the topic. On the blank line write a suitable topic sentence for the paragraph (E.2).

_____

Here is another group of sentences:

3. George washed the blackboard. He swept the floor. Robert cleaned the erasers. He dusted the desks. He emptied the wastebasket.

Which of the items below should be the topic?
a. George
b. Robert
c. George and Robert

Which of the items below best expresses what should be said about the topic?
a. swept the floor
b. dusted the desks
c. cleaned the room

Now you know the topic of the paragraph and what should be said about the topic. On the blank line write a suitable topic sentence for the paragraph (E.3).

_____

STRUCTURE EXERCISES

F. Here are some groups of questions arranged in paragraph form. Change the questions into statements. The statements will form a paragraph. Do not use *yes* or *no*. Be very careful about the verbs.

UNIT 3

Example   *Is the White House in Washington? Are there many large government buildings in the capital? Does the Congress meet in the Capitol building? Do many tourists visit Washington every year?*

The White House is in Washington. There are many large government buildings in the capital. The Congress meets in the Capitol building. Many tourists visit Washington every year.

Did you notice the two words *capital* and *capitol*? Why are they spelled differently? Why does *Capitol* begin with a capital letter?

Assignment

G. Rewrite the two groups of questions below. Change the questions into statements and write the statements in paragraph form like the example above.
After you finish the paragraphs, read them carefully to make sure you have made no mistakes in capitalization, punctuation, or spelling. Also check the form of the verbs.

1. Was the capital of the United States named for George Washington, the first President? Did he select the place for the capital in 1791? Did he hire a famous French engineer to draw plans for the city? Did Congress follow the plans? Did the government move to the capital in 1800? Did Washington slowly develop into a large and beautiful city? Is government the main business in Washington?
2. Is the White House the home of the President? Was the original building started in 1792? Did it require a long time to complete the building? Were President and Mrs. John Adams the first occupants? Did other Presidents make many changes in the White House? Is the present building very different from the first one? Do many tourists visit it every year?

Spelling

H. Here are some words that were used in this unit and in Unit 2. You should memorize the spelling of these words. Of course you should also know the meaning and pronunciation of each word.

Nouns
factory — factories
busine<u>ss</u> — busine<u>sses</u>
gover<u>nm</u>ent — gover<u>nm</u>ents
supply — supplies

NOTICE THE <u>n</u> AND <u>m</u> TOGETHER.

Adjectives
modern
di<u>ff</u>erent
famous

22

NOTICE THE i BEFORE THE e.

Verbs
bel<u>ie</u>ve — bel<u>ie</u>ves — bel<u>ie</u>ved
contain — contains — contained

Adverb
carefu<u>ll</u>y

Dividing Words Between Syllables

I. Sometimes when you are taking dictation or copying paragraphs, you come to the right side of the paper and do not have room to write a complete word. What should you do? You can divide the word and put part of it on the next line. However, you must divide the word *only between syllables.* If you are not sure about the syllables, look up the word in a dictionary. When you do not have a dictionary and you are not certain about the syllables, write all of the word on the next line.

There are several rules to learn about dividing words at the end of a line. First of all, some words should *not* be divided. Here are two rules to remember.

Rules for Dividing Words

(1) Never divide a word that has only one syllable.
Examples: *come, know, book, they*

(2) Even if a word has more than one syllable, do not divide it so that one letter stands alone.
Examples: Do *not* divide words like this: *a-lone, a-fraid, e-nough*

EXERCISE

How would you divide the following words at the end of a line? Which words would you not divide? You may use your dictionary if you are not certain of any of the words.

along   card
peculiarity   decision
evict   party
brown   beneficial
mealy   sudden

Which of the above words fit rule 1?
Which words fit rule 2?

UNIT 3

23

UNIT 3

Assignment

J. Study the following questions. They will be dictated at the next class session. You will then change the questions to statements as in assignment G.

   Are Ford cars common in the United States? Was the first Ford made by Henry Ford? Did he make his cars in Detroit? Did Detroit become famous for car factories? Is General Motors also a large company? Are Ford and General Motors the two largest car makers in the country?

Spelling Review

K. How many words do you remember from Unit 2? The spelling words from Unit 2 are used in the sentences below. Each word is spelled three ways. One way is correct and two are not correct. Cross out the incorrect words and leave the correctly spelled word in the sentence. DO NOT LOOK BACK AT UNIT 2.

1. Our (libary library libery) has a lot of good books.
2. Can you (describe discribe describ) the person who robbed you?
3. The teacher (explained explaned explanned) the paragraph.
4. When a person is sick, he sometimes has to go to a (hospittal hospitel hospital).
5. It was a (beutiful beatiful beautiful) summer day.
6. Did you (notise notice nottice) the new store on the corner?
7. Careful drivers have very few (accidents acidents accidants).
8. This is an (important impertant importent) part of the lesson.
9. This student (usualy usually usally) does his homework.
10. Please give me some (infomation infamation information) about the streets in this city.

UNIT 4

Dictation

A. Do the dictation that was assigned in the preceding unit. Change the questions to statements and write the statements in the form of a paragraph.

Review

B. In Unit 3 you wrote topic sentences for paragraphs. Here are three more paragraphs. Read the paragraphs carefully and then write a good topic sentence for each one.

1. _____
First they visited the elephants. Then they visited the lions and tigers. Next they saw the bears. Some of the bears were brown and some were black. Their last stop was at the monkey cage. The children enjoyed the monkeys most of all.

2. _____
As soon as she got to work, her boss dictated several letters. Julie typed the letters neatly and gave them to her boss to sign. The telephone rang frequently and she answered it. She had to find several letters in the files. Noon came very fast.

3. _____
Mrs. Garcia cleaned the stove and washed the kitchen floor on Saturday. She also cleaned the refrigerator inside and outside. Her daughter Anna helped her. Anna dusted the furniture in the living room and cleaned the rug with the vacuum cleaner. Then she put clean sheets on the bed and used the vacuum cleaner in the bedrooms.

ADDING DETAILS

C. You have seen that in a good paragraph all the sentences deal with one topic. Very often the topic is stated in the first sentence. The topic sentence is usually a general statement. The sentences that follow it are more specific. They add facts or details about the topic.

The topic sentence tells the reader what the paragraph is about. After this sentence the writer gives more details, to explain the topic more fully and to make it as clear as possible to the reader. A very simple example is the paragraph you read in Unit 2 about a book. Here it is again:

Example 1.   *There is a book on the desk. It is a large book. It is new. It is a chemistry book.*

The first sentence is a statement about a book. The second sentence gives you another piece of information about the book. The third sentence gives you another piece of information. The fourth sentence gives you still another piece of information. Piece by piece, each detail adds to your information about the book.

Here is another example:

Example 2.   *A secretary does various kinds of work. She takes dictation in shorthand. She uses a typewriter and other office machines. She files letters, reports, and other kinds of material. She answers the telephone and receives visitors.*

When you read the specific details, you understand much better what "various kinds of work" really means.

The next example is more like the paragraphs you usually read:

Example 3.   *Basketball is a popular sport in the United States. Many Americans prefer it to football because it is a faster game. It is played indoors throughout the winter. Basketball is especially popular in high schools. There are also many college and professional basketball teams.*

Notice how the sentences add more details about the topic. First there is a general statement about basketball. Then each sentence that follows gives another bit of information about this topic.

"List" Paragraphs

D. A paragraph that consists of a topic sentence and details like those in the examples is something like a list. It can be arranged like this:

1. There is a book on the desk.
   It is a large book.
   It is new.
   It is a chemistry book.

2. A secretary does various kinds of work.
   She takes dictation in shorthand.
   She uses a typewriter and other office machines.
   She files letters, reports, and other kinds of material.
   She answers the telephone and receives visitors.

3. Basketball is a popular sport in the United States.
Many Americans prefer it to football because it is a faster game.
It is played indoors throughout the winter.
Basketball is especially popular in high schools.
There are also many college and professional basketball teams.

In a "list" type of paragraph, more details can be added if the writer wishes. On the other hand, if he wishes to omit some of the sentences to make the paragraph shorter, it does not spoil the paragraph.

Other paragraphs that you have read are similar to these. For example:

Examples 4. *Bicycles provide a simple form of transportation. They are used for both pleasure and business. The word* bicycle *means "two wheels." The rider pedals with his feet to make the wheels move. No one knows who built the first bicycle.*

5. *Thomas A. Edison was an American inventor. He was born in Ohio in 1847. Throughout his life he worked in various technical and scientific fields. He became very successful and famous. Perhaps his most important invention was the electric light.*

Notice in these examples that all the added details are about the topic but that they give various kinds of information about the topic.

Oral Composition

E. The class will compose a paragraph orally. The paragraph will be similar to the examples you have just read. The teacher will write one of these topic sentences on the board:

1. Baseball is a popular sport in the United States.
2. In his job as stock boy at the supermarket, Edward does various things.
3. What makes a good automobile driver?
4. Fashions for men and women are not too different today.

What details can you think of to make a paragraph about the topic chosen? The teacher will call on students to give sentences orally. Each sentence should give some information about the topic. No sentence should repeat the information in another sentence. When a student gives a good sentence, the teacher will write it on the board. After the students supply several good sentences, there will be a complete paragraph on the board.

When the paragraph is finished, you are to make a copy of the paragraph to hand in. After you copy it, read it again to check the capital letters, punctuation, and spelling.

UNIT 4

COPYREADING

F. When you correct a piece of writing, you are doing *copyreading*. It is very important to learn to notice errors. Students often do not notice their own errors. You should always *copyread* your compositions before you hand them in to find any small mistakes you have made.

Need for Added Details

G. The details that are added after the first sentence make the paragraph clearer and more helpful because of the added information. Added details also make the topic more interesting to the reader.

In some paragraphs, there is another reason for adding more details. A lot depends on the topic sentence. With a certain kind of topic sentence, it is very necessary to give more information of a certain kind. Look at these two paragraphs:

Example 1.   *John is a student in my class. We often walk home together from school. John is a little older than I am. He is tall, good-looking, strong for his age, and good at sports. He is popular in school.*

Example 2.   *John is a very good student. He does his homework every night. His notebook is neat. He is always able to answer correctly when the teacher calls on him. He usually gets an excellent mark on examinations.*

The first paragraph is similar to paragraphs 1, 2, 3, 4 and 5 under D. It gives details of various kinds about John. The paragraph identifies John and gives general information about him. The topic of this paragraph is simply *John*.

Now notice that the second paragraph has a different kind of topic sentence. When you begin with a statement like "John is a very good student," it is necessary to add the kind of information that will make the reader believe what you are saying. The reader may think this is only your personal opinion about John, and he may not feel sure that your opinion is correct. You must give the reader some definite, specific information so that he can judge for himself. You must give the kind of information that will *support* your statement. This is the purpose of the added details in paragraph 2.

The purpose of this paragraph is to show that John is a very good student. After the reader reads the specific supporting sentences that tell about John's homework, his neat notebook, his ability to answer the teacher's questions, and his excellent marks on examinations, he will probably agree that John really *is* a good student.

What is the topic of paragraph 2? Of course, the paragraph is about John, but the topic sentence makes a specific kind of statement about John. The general topic is John, but the more specific topic is: *John is a good student.* Another way of saying it would be: *John's ability as a student.* Therefore, it would not be suitable to put in

Kinds of Details

sentences saying that John is tall or handsome or good at sports, for this information does not belong in this paragraph. It is irrelevant. It is right for paragraph 1 to give various kinds of information, but paragraph 2 should give only one kind of information.

Read these paragraphs:

Example 3. *Bicycles provide a simple form of transportation. They are used for both pleasure and business. The word* bicycle *means "two wheels." The rider pedals with his feet to make the wheels move. No one knows who built the first bicycle.*

Example 4. *Bicycles are very popular today. For a long time boys and girls had bicycles, but grown people seldom had them. Today more than 20 million Americans, both old and young, ride bicycles for recreation and transportation. Many communities have made special roads just for bicycling.*

Which paragraph gives only one specific kind of information about bicycles?

We can say that the topic of paragraph 3 is simply *bicycles,* meaning bicycles in general. What is the topic of paragraph 4?

H. Look again at paragraph G.1, which begins: *John is a student in my class.* As you know, this paragraph gives general information. All the sentences are about John, but the sentences give various kinds of information.

Now you are to write a similar paragraph about someone you know. The person may be in your class but doesn't have to be. Use one of these sentences for your topic sentence:

_____ is a student in my class.
_____ is one of my friends.

Then write several (four or more) sentences giving general information. You may write about this person's appearance, home, job, character, or anything else you wish. The paragraph should be similar to G.1 about John.

When you have finished your paragraph, make a neat copy to hand in. Then read it through carefully and correct any mistakes. Pay special attention to your verbs.

Assignment

UNIT 4

UNIT 4

FACT OR OPINION?

I. The kind of information in a paragraph depends on the kind of topic sentence that begins the paragraph. Some topic sentences may be statements based on judgment or opinion. Other topic sentences may be statements based on facts that can be checked and verified. Notice the difference in these two statements:

    a. The American automobile industry produced more than 8,000,000 cars in 1969.
    b. The American automobile industry produces the best cars in the world.

Sentence *a* contains a definite fact that can be checked and verified. However, sentence *b* seems to be a matter of opinion or judgment. It may be true, but it may not be true. The statement may be difficult to prove. Certainly a writer who makes such a statement will have to supply very strong supporting details to convince the reader that it is true.

2. Read the following statements. Which of these statements seem like expressions of judgment or opinion and would need strong supporting details if they were used as topic sentences for paragraphs? Put an X before these statements.

_____ 1. The Volkswagen is a small car made in Germany.
_____ 2. Henry is a clever businessman.
_____ 3. The Madison Grill is the best restaurant in town.
_____ 4. Every year more than 1,800 people are killed in motor vehicle accidents in this state.
_____ 5. You will never find better coffee than Higgins' coffee.
_____ 6. The Volkswagen is the best buy of the small imported cars.
_____ 7. The Red Cross was established in the 1860s to take care of soldiers who were sick or were wounded in war.
_____ 8. Florida is a better state for retired people than California.
_____ 9. The population of this state has increased every year for the past ten years.
_____ 10. Sir Edward Jenner was an English doctor who discovered a way to prevent smallpox.
_____ 11. Barbara Hopkins is the most popular girl in the senior class.
_____ 12. The Democrats have done a lot more for this city than the Republicans.
_____ 13. The cost of living continued to rise during the past year.
_____ 14. Heart attacks cause more deaths among men than among women.
_____ 15. People aren't as honest today as they were years ago.

Punctuation

J. You know that the period is an important punctuation mark because it indicates the end of a sentence.

The comma is another important punctuation mark. The comma is used in various ways. Here is one common way in which the comma is used.

Punctuation Rule (1): The Comma   Use a comma to separate words or expressions in a series.

Examples: *Mary bought apples, oranges, and bananas.*
Edison's ideas helped to give us the electric light, the phonograph, and moving pictures.
The man walked up the steps, through the doorway, and into the hall.

EXERCISE

Punctuate these sentences. Put in capital letters, periods, and commas where they are needed.

1. my cousin joseph is good in his school work
2. the school subjects he likes best are mathematics chemistry and physics
3. he reads a great deal
4. he prefers books on science history and biography
5. joseph is also good at sports
6. his favorite sports are volleyball basketball and football
7. he plays some kind of game every saturday and sunday afternoon
8. all these activities keep joseph very busy
9. during his vacation he plans to take a trip
10. he wants to go to philadelphia baltimore and washington

Spelling

K. 1. How well do you remember the spelling of words? The following sentences include words from the spelling lists that you have studied. Each word is spelled three ways. One way is correct and two are incorrect. Cross out the incorrect words and leave the correctly spelled word in the sentence. DO NOT LOOK BACK AT THE PRECEDING SPELLING LISTS.

UNIT 4

Review

a. The two men have (diferent different differant) ideas about politics.
b. I (usualy usally usually) take the No. 4 bus.
c. Do you (believe beleive beilive) everything you hear?
d. The pollution was caused by the large number of (factory factorie's factories) in the area.
e. She was wearing a (beautiful beutiful buetifull) new dress.
f. Robert Redford is a (fameous famuos famous) movie star.
g. Please check your paragraph (carfully carefully carefuly).
h. Helen is a young woman with (modern modren moddern) ideas.
i. The (goverment governemt government) collects taxes from the people.
j. I am going to take some flowers to my friend in the (hospittal hopital hospital).

New Words

2. Here are some words that were used in this unit or in preceding units. You should memorize the spelling of these words. Of course you should also know their meaning and pronunciation.

Nouns
country — countries
industry — industries
company — companies
opinion — opinions

Adjectives
popular

NOTICE THE DOUBLE LETTERS.
di<u>ff</u>icult
similar (to)

Verbs
produce — produces — produced

NOTICE THE DOUBLE LETTERS IN THE PAST TENSE.
prefer — prefers — prefe<u>rr</u>ed

Adverb
probably

L. Study the following questions. Learn the spelling of new words. Be prepared for dictation of the questions. Then you will change them into statements and form a paragraph. Copyread the paragraph carefully before handing it in.

Assignment

UNIT 4

Dictation

Are more people traveling today than ever before? Do cars, buses, and planes make traveling much easier and faster than it was years ago? Do people have more time and more money than in former times? Do they have more information about all parts of the world? Does the world seem smaller than it used to seem?

Game

M. Here is a game that will give you practice in vocabulary and spelling. Read the following directions carefully.

Directions: Take out a piece of paper to write on. The teacher will choose a word and write the letters of the word on the chalkboard like this:

    d   e
    e   r
    c   a
    l   l
    a   c
    r   e
    e   d

The teacher will then write the letters of the word backward as in column 2. You are to write words beginning with the letters in the first column and ending with the letters in the second column (*date,* for example). You will have five minutes to complete this game. The student who has the most words, correctly spelled, is the winner. You will exchange papers with one of your neighbors for correction. The teacher will help if anyone is unsure of a correct spelling of a word.

UNIT 5

Dictation

A. Do the dictation and write the paragraph that was assigned in the preceding unit.

SUPPORTING SENTENCES

B. As you have seen, the kind of statement made in the topic sentence determines what kind of information should be included in the paragraph. We say that the topic sentence *controls* the paragraph.

The sentences that add details are called *supporting sentences*. Different kinds of topic sentences require different kinds of supporting details. Sometimes the details make the topic sentence clearer or more interesting. Sometimes the details show why the topic sentence is true.

EXERCISE

Here is a topic sentence, followed by several other sentences. Some of the sentences support the topic sentence, but some do not. Put an X in front of the sentences that do *not* support the topic sentence.

a. *Topic sentence*: The increasing number of car accidents is a serious problem.

　　_____ 1. The number of accidents last year increased 10 per cent over the year before.
　　_____ 2. One cause is the great increase in the number of cars on the road.
　　_____ 3. Ownership of a car involves a lot of expense.
　　_____ 4. There would be fewer accidents if drivers were more careful.
　　_____ 5. A car owner must have a license.
　　_____ 6. Many drivers do not pay attention to the speed laws.

Now do the same thing with the next sentences.

b. *Topic sentence*: There are many medicines for a cold, but few of them are effective.

　　_____ 1. People often catch cold in the winter or spring.

34

UNIT 5

_____ 2. If you have a cold, your friends will suggest medicines that they say are good.
_____ 3. Pharmacies have dozens of "remedies" for colds.
_____ 4. A person with a cold feels very uncomfortable.
_____ 5. Doctors doubt the value of these "remedies."
_____ 6. Doctors usually say that the most effective thing to do is to stay in bed, keep warm, and drink lots of liquids.
_____ 7. People often catch cold from contact with a person who has a cold.

Oral Composition

C. The class will again compose a paragraph orally. This time you will write about Washington, D.C. You had some information about Washington in a previous unit. What do you remember about Washington?

The teacher will write on the board this topic sentence: "Washington is the capital of the United States." You are to give sentences that provide additional details. With this kind of topic sentence, you may give details of various kinds. No sentence should repeat the information in another sentence. When a student gives a good sentence, the teacher will write it on the board. After students give several good sentences, there will be a complete paragraph on the board.

When the paragraph is finished, you will make a copy of it to hand in. Be careful about capital letters, punctuation, and spelling.

PUNCTUATION EXERCISE

D. Punctuate the following paragraph. Put in capital letters, periods, and commas where they are needed.

more tourists are visiting foreign countries every year the most popular months for travel are june july and august tourists are interested in the scenery the people and the customs of each country they visit they are also interested in buying things they buy articles for themselves they also buy presents for their relatives and friends they buy jewelry perfume clothes pictures and many other things

35

UNIT 5

ORDER IN SENTENCES

E. You have seen that a good paragraph has a single topic and that all the sentences in the paragraph are about that topic. If a sentence is not about the topic, it is irrelevant. Different kinds of topic sentences require different kinds of supporting sentences.

Another important point about paragraphs is that the sentences must follow each other in good order. Even if all the sentences relate to one topic, they will be confusing to the reader if they do not follow each other in a certain order. You have already seen (in Unit 1) how important this is when paragraphs are supposed to follow time order. Notice how confusing this paragraph is.

Example 1. *George liked one of them. The librarian gave him three books to look at. George visited the library. He checked the book out and took it home with him. He asked for a book to read.*

You can see that because the sentences are mixed up, this paragraph does not make sense. Now read it again with the sentences in order. Of course, this paragraph uses time order.

Example 1a. *George visited the library. He asked for a book to read. The librarian gave him three books to look at. George liked one of them. He checked the book out and took it home with him.*

The same thing is true with paragraphs that should have logical order. As you know, *logical* means that the sentences should be clear and easy for the reader to understand. The sentences should move from one idea to another so smoothly that the reader can follow the writer's thinking.

Look at this paragraph:

Example 2. *One is to chew our food, which is then easy to swallow and digest. The second use is to help us talk. There are two main uses for teeth.*

This paragraph will seem familiar to you because you have read the sentences before, in Unit 1. You can see, however, that the sentences are not in good order. Now here is the order in which the sentences appeared in the original paragraph:

Example 2a. *There are two main uses for teeth. One is to chew our food, which is then easy to swallow and digest. The second use is to help us talk.*

Compare these sentences with those above and notice how clear example 2a is compared with example 2. This is what we mean by *logical* order. It is the kind of order that makes information clear to the reader.

UNIT 5

The paragraphs below are similar. How should the sentences be rearranged to put them in better order? First decide which sentence should be the first one. Then decide on the second and third sentences.

Example 3. *The sweet orange is the kind commonly grown and eaten in the United States. There are two kinds of oranges. The other kind is called the bitter, or sour, orange.*

Example 4. *In a cafeteria you carry your food on a tray. You are also served in a restaurant, where you sit at a table instead of at a counter. Three kinds of eating places are common in cities. In a lunch room you sit at a counter and someone serves you.*

F. The paragraphs that follow are not in good order. Underline the sentence that you think is the topic sentence, the one that should begin the paragraph.

EXERCISE

1. Trees give us fruit and nuts to eat. We use their wood to make furniture and buildings. Much of our paper is made from wood. Trees are very important in our lives. In winter we burn wood to keep us warm and in summer trees give us cool shade.

2. She had great difficulty getting a medical education. The medical schools did not want a woman student. Finally a medical college at Geneva, New York, accepted her. Elizabeth Blackwell was the first woman doctor in the United States. She was graduated in 1849.

3. If money is lost or stolen, there is little chance of getting it back. If a blank check is lost, no harm is done. Using checks is safer and more convenient than carrying money. If a signed check is lost, the bank can be told not to cash it. In addition, a check can safely be mailed.

4. Before someone had the idea of stamps, sending a letter was very inconvenient. The person who thought of the paper clip has helped everyone who has worked in an office since then. Most of our small, common conveniences came into existence because someone in the past had a bright idea. And the person who got the idea of the safety pin made another small but important contribution.

5. Overpopulation is one of our greatest problems. It is a world problem as well as a problem of concern to our own country. Protection of the environment is another problem that affects all of us. Of the many problems of the modern world, three stand out in importance. This problem is closely related to the problem of overpopulation. Race relations is another of our country's most important problems.

UNIT 5

COHERENCE

G. When sentences in a paragraph follow each other in good order, we say the paragraph has *coherence*. The word *cohere* means *to stick together*.

H. Rewrite three of the paragraphs in exercise F. You may choose any three. Begin each paragraph with the topic sentence you selected and omit this sentence from inside the paragraph. When you finish writing the paragraphs, read them through to check the capitalization, punctuation, and spelling.

Assignment

STRUCTURE PATTERN

I. 1. This exercise will help you tell when sentences are complete and when they are incomplete.

As you know, every sentence must have a subject and a verb (a correct verb, of course). The verb usually follows the subject.

> The boy ran.
> The children yelled.
> The girl smiled.

Many sentences are not as simple as these. In these sentences the verbs (*run, yell, smile*) do not require an object or any following words. But very often other words do follow these verbs. For example:

> The boy ran to the corner.
> The boy ran after the bus.
> The children yelled at their friends.
> The children yelled loudly.
> The girl smiled happily.
> The girl smiled at her boy friend.

Some verbs must have an object. You cannot say *The girl combed*. The girl must comb *something*. Many verbs are like this.

Wrong:	The girl combed.	*Right*:	The girl combed her hair.
	The man bought.		The man bought a new hat.
	The boys saw.		The boys saw an accident.
	A thief took.		A thief took my bicycle.
	Joseph likes.		Joseph likes sports.

UNIT 5

For the present, we will say that everything that comes after the verb is the *complement*. Then we can fit sentences into a frame like this:

Subject	Verb	Complement
1. The boy	ran.	
2. The boy	ran	after the bus.
3. The children	yelled.	
4. The children	yelled	loudly.
5. The girl	smiled.	
6. The girl	smiled	at her boyfriend.
7. The girl	combed	her hair.
8. The man	bought	a new hat.
9. A thief	took	my bicycle.
10. Joseph	likes	sports.

EXERCISE

2. For practice, write these sentences in the frame below.

   a. We are in English class.
   b. The class meets twice a week.
   c. Our teacher gives us exercises to write.
   d. Mr. Smith has a new Chevrolet.
   e. He parks his car behind the building.

Subject	Verb	Complement

EXERCISE

3. Here are some groups of words; some are complete sentences and some are incomplete.

   a. She reads the newspaper every day.
   b. Studied the lesson last night.
   c. A letter for you.

UNIT 5

    d. Most nouns have two forms.
    e. A long trip on a bus.
    f. He is my brother.
    g. Rains every day.
    h. My grandfather in Boston.
    i. Came for a visit.
    j. The weather was beautiful.

You are to do this exercise in three steps. Follow the directions.

Directions:
  Step 1. Read each group of words. Mark each group that forms a complete sentence. Copy the sentences in the following frame. Include the letter (*a, b,* etc.) of the sentence. Omit the groups of words that do not form a sentence. When you finish, the teacher will check the sentences with you.

Subject	Verb	Complement

  Step 2. Go back and look at the groups of words that are not sentences. Write them in the frame below. Include the letter. Because they are not sentences, you will have some blank spaces. In some cases, the subject will be missing. In some cases, the verb or the complement may be missing.

Subject	Verb	Complement

  Step 3. Now can you add missing parts (subject, verb, or complement) to these groups of words and make them complete sentences?

UNIT 5

Spelling

J. Here are some words that were used in this unit. You should memorize the spelling of these words. Of course you should also know their meaning and pronunciation.

Nouns
expense — expenses
license — licenses
medicine — medicines

NOTICE THAT ph SOUNDS LIKE f
<u>ph</u>armacy — <u>ph</u>armacies

Adjectives
NOTICE THE SILENT LETTERS
forei<u>g</u>n
familiar
convenient

Verbs
THIS VERB IS IRREGULAR
buy — buys — bought
NOTICE THE DOUBLE LETTERS
a<u>cc</u>ept — a<u>cc</u>epts — a<u>cc</u>epted

Adverb
NOTICE THE DOUBLE LETTERS
fina<u>ll</u>y

Idioms
pay attention — pays attention — paid attention
catch cold — catches cold — caught cold

EXERCISE

In each of the following groups of words, one word has been misspelled. Spell it correctly in the blank space. (Each of the misspelled words has come from the lists of spelling words that you have studied.)

Example: *meaning, diferent, something, mistake*   *different*

a. correction, amount, aciddent, increase   _____
b. winner, hospitel, invention, convenient   _____
c. notise, magazine, teacher, various   _____
d. details, period, oppinion, language   _____
e. underline, mention, heavy, usally   _____
f. governent, journey, question, valuable   _____
g. sentence, paragraph, bussiness, purpose   _____
h. recreation, specific, sometimes, similiar   _____
i. problem, consequently, beleive, doctor   _____
j. suply, frequently, dictation, useful   _____

UNIT 5

K. Study the following paragraph carefully. Notice the spelling, capitalization, punctuation, and the structure of the sentences. The teacher will dictate this paragraph in a different manner. Instead of saying all the words, the teacher will substitute the word *blank* for some of the words. You are to place a blank where indicated. After the dictation is over, you are to fill the blanks with the proper word.

Assignment

Example: *The common* _____*cold*_____ *is familiar to everyone.*

Dictation

The common cold is familiar to everyone. People often catch cold in the winter or spring. They may also catch cold at other times of the year. A person with a bad cold usually buys some kind of medicine. Pharmacies have many medicines for a cold. However, doctors say that these medicines do not help very much. They say that a person with a bad cold should stay in bed, keep warm, and drink a lot of liquids.

UNIT 6

Dictation

A. Do the dictation that was assigned in the preceding unit and then fill in the blanks. Your teacher will explain.

COHERENCE

B. You have seen that in a clear paragraph the sentences must follow each other in good order. If they do not, the paragraph becomes mixed up and confusing. The supporting sentences must be related to the topic sentence and also *to each other*. If the ideas are to be clearly understood by the reader, there must be close connection between the sentences.

When you read paragraphs, you may not be conscious of how closely related the sentences are. You probably think about the ideas and do not notice how the sentences are connected. If they were not closely connected, however, you would have difficulty in following the author's ideas.

There are many ways in which sentences are connected with each other. First we will look at one of the most common ways. Notice the underlined words in this paragraph:

Example 1. *People are thinking now about traveling to the moon. Perhaps you or your children will someday make a trip to the moon. Such a trip is no longer just a wild, impossible dream. If you go to the moon, you will have to wear a space suit. A space suit is necessary to protect you from the intense heat and the intense cold on the moon. The extreme heat and cold result from the very thin air on the moon.*

Key Words Repeated

The underlined words serve as connections, or links, between the sentences in the paragraph. These words carry the ideas from one sentence to the next. In these sentences, the links consist chiefly of key words which are repeated. This is a common and basic kind of link, particularly in easy paragraphs.

As sentences and paragraphs become more advanced and difficult, there is less repetition of the same words and more use of other kinds of links. Another kind of link is illustrated in the next example.

UNIT 6

Example 2.   <u>Your space suit</u> will help you in another way. <u>It</u> will have a special cover for your head. <u>It</u> will have tanks of air. People from the earth cannot live in the thin air of the moon.

Pronouns

In this paragraph, the writer, instead of repeating key words, has used the pronoun *it* to substitute for certain words. This is done to avoid using the same words again and again. When the same words are repeated too frequently, they become monotonous. Pronouns give variety to writing. The use of pronouns is another very common kind of link between sentences.

Of course, *it* is not the only pronoun used in this way. The other personal pronouns (*he, him, she, her, they, them,* etc.) are used in the same way. Here are two examples showing the use of *he, him* and *they*:

Example 3.   As a child, <u>George Washington Carver</u> was unusual. <u>He</u> was very interested in the things around <u>him</u>. <u>He</u> was always experimenting with plants.

Example 4.   When <u>Carver</u> went to the university, <u>he</u> was at the top of his class. <u>The teachers</u> liked <u>him</u> because he was such a good student. <u>They</u> helped <u>him</u> get a job as a teacher when <u>he</u> graduated.

The repetition of key words and the use of pronouns are two of the basic kinds of links between sentences. You will study and use other kinds of links as you continue to practice writing compositions.

When you are reading, it is correct for you to give most of your attention to the ideas, but when you are writing, you must also be careful about the connections between your sentences. These connections are like the links in a chain. You will remember that *cohere* means *to stick together*. The links hold the sentences together so that they form a chain.

EXERCISE

C. This exercise will give you practice in seeing links between sentences. Underline the personal pronouns in these paragraphs. Put two lines below the word or group of words that each pronoun refers to.

1. Green plants make their own food. They use sunlight, which is a form of energy. With sunlight they are able to put water and carbon dioxide together to make sugar.

UNIT 6

2. Clara Barton, who grew up in Massachusetts, organized the American Red Cross. During the Civil War she helped wounded soldiers on the battlefield. After the war she spent some time in Europe. There she learned about the International Red Cross and realized the need for such an organization in the United States.

3. The small part of the United States called the District of Columbia was named in honor of Christopher Columbus. It is between Maryland and Virginia. The District is not part of any state. It has the same boundaries as Washington, the nation's capital. It belongs to the whole country.

4. Common matches are small and may not seem very important. But they save a great deal of time and trouble. Before the days of matches, people had a great deal of difficulty in lighting a fire. They often went a long distance to borrow hot coals instead of trying to start a fire for themselves.

5. Thomas Jefferson was the third President of the United States. He was famous even before this, for he wrote the Declaration of Independence. Jefferson had a great many interests. He liked science and music, and he was a good architect. Because he was interested in education, he founded the University of Virginia.

Punctuation

D. Here is another punctuation exercise. When you do the exercise, remember this additional rule about using commas.

Punctuation Rule (2): The Comma

Use a comma after the word *however* when it begins a sentence.
Use a comma before and after the word *however* when it occurs inside a sentence.
Use a comma before *however* when it occurs at the end of a sentence.

Examples: *In winter this city is cold.*
However, in summer it is very hot.
In summer, however, it is very hot.
In summer it is very hot, however.

EXERCISE

Punctuate the following sentences. You need to pay attention to capital letters, commas, and periods.

45

UNIT 6

1. in some countries the climate is very similar in all areas
2. in the united states however the climate varies
3. florida minnesota and oregon have different climates
4. california is different from maine
5. in the western part of the country there are high mountains that are very cold
6. there are also large deserts where it is very hot
7. the climate in texas is different from that in connecticut
8. however western texas arizona and new mexico are similar in climate
9. no matter what kind of climate you like, you can probably find it in the united states

How many words did you capitalize? _____
How many commas did you put in? _____
How many periods did you put in? _____

Relevant and Irrelevant Sentences

E. Read the following paragraphs and notice the topic sentence of each. Some of the paragraphs contain only relevant material, but others include material that is irrelevant. Put an X in front of the paragraphs that you think include irrelevant material. Underline the irrelevant material.

EXERCISE

_____ 1. Traffic has become a serious problem in this area. In the past three years the number of cars here has doubled. It is expensive to own a car. Some of the streets are too narrow for the amount of traffic they have to carry. Many drivers do not follow the rules of sensible driving, for they drive much faster than they should and frequently they fail to signal when they are going to turn.

_____ 2. English is now almost an international language. It is spoken by pilots and airport control operators on all the airways of the world. More than 70 per cent of the world's mail is written in English. In international business English is used more than any other language.

46

UNIT 6

_____ 3. The tiny organisms that cause disease are probably man's most dangerous enemies. They are so small that they can be seen only with a microscope. These tiny organisms are called *germs* or *microbes*. For thousands of years people did not know what caused disease. Some people believed that disease was caused by an evil spirit inside a sick person's body. Chicken pox is a common children's disease.

_____ 4. New words are constantly being added to the English language. One way we create new words is by combining words from other languages. For instance, *television* comes from *tele*, which means *far* in Greek, and *video*, which means *to see* in Latin. Some new words are simply invented, such as *kleenex* and *nylon*. Another way in which new words are formed is by combining old words; examples are *lipstick* and *cheeseburger*.

Spelling

F. 1. Here are some words that have been used in these units. You should memorize the spelling of these words. You should also know their meaning and pronunciation.

NOTICE THE DOUBLE LETTERS.

Nouns
diffi̲culty — diffi̲culties
remedy — remedies
co̲nnection — co̲nnections
traffi̲c — *no plural*

Adjectives
dangerous
expensive
various

Verbs
co̲nnect — co̲nnects — co̲nnected
lose — loses — lost

THIS VERB IS IRREGULAR.

Adverb
frequently

47

UNIT 6

REVIEW EXERCISE

2. The blanks in these sentences are to be filled with words that you have had in spelling lists. The first letter of the needed word is given. How many words can you complete correctly?

Example: *Isn't it time to return this book to the l ibrary   ?*

a. Mrs. Jackson became sick. Her husband took her to the h_____.
b. Mrs. Jackson did not want to go there. She was worried that it would be too e_____.
c. Mr. Jackson said that her health was more i_____ than money.
d. On his way home, Mr. Jackson saw a bad a_____ in the street.
e. In his o_____, one of the cars was going too fast.
f. A policeman asked Mr. Jackson to d_____ what he saw.
g. The rest of the way home Mr. Jackson drove very c_____.
h. He did not want anything to happen because he remembered that he did not have his driver's l_____ with him.
i. When he got home, he had a headache. He took some m_____ for it.
j. He looked in the refrigerator, but it did not c_____ much to eat.
k. Since he was hungry, he went to the store and b_____ some food for his supper.
l. The food was good, but he p_____ his wife's cooking.
m. In the evening Mr. Jackson went to see his wife. He n_____ that she seemed much better.

Assignment

G. Here is a paragraph that is familiar to you. Study it carefully. Be sure you can spell all the words. Be prepared for dictation of this paragraph, with blanks, similar to the dictation in the previous unit.

Using checks is safer and more convenient than carrying money. If money is lost or stolen, there is little chance of getting it back. If a blank check is lost, no harm is done. If a signed check is lost, the bank can be told not to cash it. In addition, a check can safely be mailed.

UNIT 7

Dictation

A. Do the dictation assigned in the preceding unit. Fill in the blanks.

Choosing Topic Sentences

B. 1. Look at the example paragraph. This paragraph does not have a topic sentence. Following the paragraph there are three sentences. Put an X before the sentence that you think would be the best topic sentence for this paragraph. Remember that the sentence you choose should come first in the paragraph.

Example a.   *He went to Cleveland, Chicago, and Minneapolis. Then he went to Seattle, San Francisco, and Los Angeles. From there he went to Dallas and Atlanta, and then back to New York.*

    _____ (1) Mr. Harrison saw many interesting things on his trip.
    _____ (2) Mr. Harrison traveled from Chicago to Seattle.
    _____ (3) Mr. Harrison traveled around the United States.

Which sentence did you choose and why did you choose it?
Sentence (1) is not a good choice because the paragraph is not about the things Mr. Harrison saw. Of course, he must have seen interesting things, but the paragraph does not say anything about them. them. The paragraph mentions only places. Sentence (2) is not a good choice because it includes only part of the information in the paragraph. Sentence (3) is the best choice for a topic sentence because it gives the general idea of the whole paragraph.
Now do the exercise.

EXERCISE

2. Choose the best topic sentence for each paragraph and mark it with an X.

a.   In the winter it is cold, and it snows and rains a lot. In the spring it is rainy and windy. The summers are very hot. The fall is cool and pleasant.
    _____ (1) This part of the country has a mild climate.
    _____ (2) The seasons in this part of the country are very different from each other.
    _____ (3) This part of the country has good weather in the fall.

UNIT 7

b. He swept the floor and emptied the wastebaskets. He washed the chalkboards and beat the erasers against each other to get out the chalk dust. He dusted all the desks. Then he put the broom, pail, and cleaning rags in the closet in the hall.
    _____ (1) The man who does the cleaning here is a good worker.
    _____ (2) The man did a good cleaning job.
    _____ (3) The janitor did a good job of cleaning the classroom.

c. The yak is an animal about the size of a small cow. The people of Tibet use it to carry large and small loads. They drink its milk, eat its meat for food, and weave its fur into cloth.
    _____ (1) The Tibetan people depend upon the yak in several ways.
    _____ (2) The yak lives in Tibet.
    _____ (3) The yak is an important means of transportation in Tibet.

d. Blue is a color that means sadness or coldness to many people. Most people think of yellow as a bright, cheerful color. People often say they "see red" when they are angry.
    _____ (1) People say strange things.
    _____ (2) To some people the color red means anger.
    _____ (3) To many people colors have certain meanings.

e. First she read the story. She looked up the meaning of new words in the dictionary. Then she learned the spelling of the words. Finally she wrote the answers to the questions in the exercises.
    _____ (1) Helen always studies her lessons carefully.
    _____ (2) Helen studied the new lesson carefully.
    _____ (3) Helen is a good student.

Kinds of Paragraphs: Review

C. Read these paragraphs:

1. Thomas A. Edison was one of the world's great inventors. His inventions have come into almost every part of our lives. When we pick up a telephone, we are using some of his ideas. When we turn on an electric light, we are benefiting by his ideas. When we put a record on a phonograph or watch a movie, we are enjoying the results of his ideas. His inventions had an important effect on the whole field of electricity.

2. Thomas A. Edison was an American inventor. He was born in Ohio in 1847. Throughout his life he worked in various technical and scientific fields. He became very successful and famous. Perhaps his most important invention was the electric light.

    Now turn back to page 28 and look again at the two paragraphs about John. The paragraphs about Edison are similar in some ways to the paragraphs about John.

a. Which paragraph about Edison is similar to paragraph 1 about John? _____
b. Which paragraph about Edison is similar to paragraph 2 about John? _____
c. Why did you mark these the way you did? Can you explain?

Punctuation

D. Punctuate the following paragraph. You need to pay attention to capital letters, commas, and periods.

many of our vegetables and fruits came from distant places. the white potato is one of our common foods It is sometimes called the Irish potato However it is not Irish. it came from south america. the Spanish found the Indians growing potatoes in the high mountains of peru and colombia. in these high places it was too cold for corn or wheat to grow The Spanish took potatoes back to spain with them From spain potatoes were taken to austria italy germany and many other countries. finally the potato plant reached the united states

How many words did you capitalize? _____
How many periods did you put in? _____
How many commas did you put in? _____

E. You studied the importance of supporting sentences in Unit 5.B. In this exercise you are to write a paragraph beginning with the topic sentence given and using *some* of the sentences that follow it. Not all of the additional sentences are suitable as supporting sentences. You must decide which sentences are relevant. Read all the sentences and then follow the directions that come after them.

Assignment

Topic sentence
   Air conditioning is important in modern business and industry.

EXERCISE:
Relevance

Additional sentences
1. It controls the temperature, moisture, cleanliness, and movement of indoor air.
2. Air conditioning improves the efficiency of office workers.
3. Some people do not mind hot weather.
4. In factories, the making of various products is helped by control of the air.

UNIT 7

5. The temperature is controlled in factories that make metal products, for metals expand when the temperature rises and contract when the temperature falls.
6. Factories that make cloth use air conditioning to control moisture in the air.
7. Air conditioning can make life more comfortable for people who suffer from hay fever.
8. The food industry uses air conditioning to keep the air clean, in addition to controlling temperature and moisture.
9. Many people use air conditioning for at least one room in their home during hot weather.

Directions: Do the above assignment in three steps:
(1) Cross out the sentences that do not support the topic sentence.
(2) Copy the topic sentence and the relevant supporting sentences in paragraph form. Copy the sentences in the same order in which they occur.
(3) After you have copied the sentences, read your paragraph and correct any mistakes in spelling, capitalization, or punctuation. Did you indent the first line of the paragraph?

Spelling

F. 1. Here are some words that have been used in these units. You should memorize the spelling of these words. You should also know their meaning and pronunciation.

Nouns
disease — diseases
NOTICE THAT ph SOUNDS LIKE f   telephone — telephones
weather — *no plural*

Adjectives
favorite
interesting
NOTICE THE DOUBLE LETTERS   necessary
successful

Verbs
organize — organizes — organized
THIS VERB IS IRREGULAR   write — writes — wrote

Adverb
always

UNIT 7

EXERCISE

2. Your spelling lists have included several words ending in *y*. Write the plural of these words.

a. company _____   e. industry _____

b. country _____   f. pharmacy _____

c. difficulty _____   g. remedy _____

d. factory _____   h. supply _____

Now here are some words that have occurred in these units but have not been included in your spelling lists. How would you write the plurals?

i. activity _____   m. embassy _____

j. boundary _____   n. enemy _____

k. city _____   o. history _____

l. dictionary _____   p. university _____

3. Perhaps you did not notice it, but in all these words there was a consonant before the *y*. There is a useful rule for the spelling of such words. Here it is:

If a word ends in *y* preceded by a consonant, form the plural by changing *y* to *i* and adding *es*.

Spelling Rule (1)

Vocabulary Game

G. This is the same game that you played once before. The teacher will write the following word in two columns like this:

<pre>
p   d
r   n
e   e
t   t
e   e
n   r
d   p
</pre>

You are to write words beginning with the letters in the first column and ending with the letters in the second column. It does not matter how many letters are in your words so long as they begin with the first letter in the first column and end with the letter in the second column. You will have five minutes to complete this. If you have time

53

UNIT 7

to write more than one word for each set of letters, write as many as you have time for. The student who has the most words, correctly spelled, is the winner. Exchange papers with your neighbors for correction. The teacher will help if anyone is unsure of a correct spelling of a word.

Dividing Words Between Syllables

H. You have learned two rules (Unit 3) for dividing words at the end of a line when you are copying material, taking dictation, or writing a composition. What are the two rules?

Another point to remember is that you should not divide a word so that only two letters come at the end of the line or are carried over to the next line. Perhaps the easiest way to remember this is to express the rule this way:

Rule for Dividing Words (3)

Do not divide a word of five or fewer letters.
Examples: Do *NOT* divide words like this: *on-ly, ma-ny, of-ten, hap-py.*

If you are uncertain about a short word, do not divide it. Put it all on the next line.

Assignment

I. Study the following paragraph. Notice the capitalization, punctuation, and spelling, as well as the order of the sentences. Your teacher will dictate this paragraph but will change the order of the sentences. After you write what the teacher dictates, you will rewrite the paragraph, putting the sentences in the correct order.

Dictation

Every city in the country has traffic problems. The number of cars increases every year. Many drivers do not drive carefully. Such drivers frequently cause accidents. They drive much faster than they should and often they do not signal when they are going to turn. They make traffic dangerous even for careful drivers.

UNIT 8

Dictation

A. Do the dictation that was assigned in the previous unit. Rewrite the paragraph placing the sentences in the proper order.

COMPLETENESS OF PARAGRAPHS

B. You have learned that a good expository paragraph has unity (the sentences deal with a single topic) and coherence (the sentences are linked together and follow each other in good order).

Another important point about a paragraph is that it must be *complete*. The example will illustrate what this means.

Example 1. *In recent years American clothes-washing customs have greatly changed. Before World War II most clothing was washed by hand or by wringer-type washing machines. After the war, however, three related developments changed the washing of clothes. First, in the late 1940s industry introduced phosphate detergents, which began to take the place of soap products. Automatic washing machines also came in.*

The third sentence of this paragraph says that *three* developments changed the washing of clothes. The reader therefore expects to find these three reasons in the paragraph. However, the paragraph gives only *two* reasons: (1) industry introduced phosphate detergents, which began to take the place of soap products, and (2) new automatic washing machines. What about the third development? The reader is left wondering about it. Because the third development is missing, this paragraph is incomplete.

If a sentence tells the reader that there are three developments, or reasons, or causes, for something, then all three of them must be given. A similar point is that if the paragraph mentions *many* developments (or reasons, causes, etc.), one or two is not enough.

Now read example 1 in its complete form:

Example 1a. *In recent years American clothes-washing customs have greatly changed. Before World War II most clothing was washed by hand or by wringer-type machines. After the war, however, three related developments changed the washing of clothes. First, in the late 1940s industry introduced phosphate detergents, which began to take the place of soap products. Automatic washing machines also*

UNIT 8

came in. Along with these came new synthetic fabrics, which were adapted for washing with the new detergents in the new washing machines.

EXERCISE

C. Examine the following paragraphs for completeness. If you do not feel that they are complete, be ready to explain what is wrong and what is needed to complete them.

1. The bicycle has affected American life in at least four important ways. The popularity of bicycles at the end of the last century led to the improvements of roads, for people wanted smoother roads to ride on. It increased the need for standardized parts, so that all makes of bicycles could be repaired more easily. It also helped to bring about a sensible change in dress for women, for it was impossible to ride a bicycle in the long, wide skirts that were fashionable at that time.

2. Because smoking is now recognized as harmful to health, numerous measures are being taken to discourage people from doing it. In some countries a written statement appears on each package of cigarettes to warn people that smoking may be dangerous to their health. In spite of everything, however, smoking is increasing in all countries of the world. The number of smokers and the amount of money spent on smoking continue to grow.

3. The number of foreign visitors to Asia is increasing for several reasons. One is that jet planes make it easier to get there than it used to be. Another is that Asian countries now have more and better hotels than they used to have. Good hotels attract tourists who have plenty of money to spend. These tourists spend considerable amounts of money shopping for things to take home with them.

SENTENCE LINKS

D. 1. Sentences are linked together in various ways. You have had examples of two ways: the repetition of key words and the use of personal pronouns.

Personal pronouns have more than one form. When a pronoun is the subject of a sentence, you use the subject form. When a pronoun is the object of a verb, you usually use the object form. Here are the two forms for review.

UNIT 8

	Subject Form	Object Form
Singular	I	me
	you	you
	he	him
	she	her
	it	it
Plural	we	us
	you	you
	they	them

Examples: *I saw Betty. Betty saw me.*
You saw Betty. Betty saw you.
He saw Betty. Betty saw him.
She saw Betty. Betty saw her.

2. Pronouns also have another form. Read the next examples and notice the underlined words. The pronouns become adjectives.

Examples: a. *Maxine was late for work. Her car broke down.*
b. *Martin Luther King was a great American leader. His fight for civil rights made him famous.*
c. *Migrant workers are people who move from place to place. Their children rarely go to school.*
d. *That door always squeaks. Its hinges need some oil.*

Possessive Adjectives

The underlined words are *possessive* adjectives. They are another common link between sentences.

Here are the subject pronouns and the corresponding possessive adjectives:

	Subject Form	Possessive Form
Singular	I	my
	you	your
	he	his
	she	her
	it	its
Plural	we	our
	you	your
	they	their

Examples: *I live near here. My house is on Mercer Street.*
You need a new tire. Your right front tire is very bad.
He is a good student. His favorite subject is history.
She is a pretty brunette. Her hair is black and her eyes are brown.
It is an old house. Its furnace needs repair.

UNIT 8

> We go to the beach in summer. <u>Our</u> friends go with us.
> They like to go to the beach. <u>Their</u> favorite sport is swimming.

EXERCISE

3. Use a possessive adjective in the blanks.

a. Joseph bought some ice cream.
   I shared the ice cream.

   I shared _____ ice cream.

b. Mrs. Jackson has a good washing machine.
   I use the washing machine.

   I use _____ washing machine.

c. I have a catcher's mitt.
   The other boys use the mitt.

   The other boys use _____ mitt.

d. Paul and Richard bought some new records.
   Henry listened to the records.

   Henry listened to _____ records.

e. Anne and I bought tickets for the concert, but we could not go.
   Mary and Betty used the tickets.

   Mary and Betty used _____ tickets.

EXERCISE

4. This exercise will provide practice in recognizing the possessive form. Underline the possessive adjectives in the following sentences. Put two lines under the word or group of words that each possessive modifies.

Model: <u>My</u> <u><u>cousin</u></u> borrowed two books from me last week.

a. She wasn't satisfied with her living room and decided to change it completely.
b. The parcel came back from the post office with its outer wrapping torn and its contents broken.
c. To his horror, he saw a rattlesnake near his outstretched foot.
d. The children were busy doing their arithmetic homework.
e. The dogs ran swiftly. There was no sound except the soft padding of their feet.
f. Tod and Mary looked at an old New England farmhouse. Its grassy yard was shaded by a sugar maple tree.
g. Our father was annoyed because John and I were late for dinner. He told us to do our lessons and get in our beds.

h. My grandmother is getting old. Her hair is almost white.
i. His hat perched on the top of his head, the boy stood watching us.
j. They threw their arms around our necks and thanked us for saving their lives.

EXERCISE

5. Fill the blanks with the correct subject or possessive form.

a. She is a famous singer. _____ records are very popular.
b. These students do good work. They always do the assignments and _____ work is very neat.
c. Anne is a well-dressed girl. She doesn't spend a lot of money on clothes, but _____ taste is very good.
d. We may move to another part of the city. _____ are too far away from _____ friends and relatives.
e. You were visiting _____ girl friend last night, weren't you? I saw _____ car in front of _____ house.
f. George did well on his last job. _____ has a very good letter of recommendation from _____ boss.
g. I often have to buy gloves. Because I am so careless, _____ frequently leave _____ gloves in restaurants or theaters.
h. Men used to wear conservative clothing. Now it seems that _____ are going in for bright colors in _____ clothes.
i. My two children are quite different in their interests. _____ daughter Monica is fond of music, but _____ brother Jerry is interested in only one thing—baseball.
j. My mother is an excellent cook, and fortunately my wife is very good at cooking, too. But in my opinion, _____ apple pie is not quite as good as _____ mother's pie.

Finding Errors in Grammar

E. You have had practice in correcting sentences by putting in capital letters, periods, and commas. Now you will have practice in correcting the grammar of sentences. Each of the sentences in this exercise contains *one* error in grammar. Correct the sentences in the same way that the examples are corrected.

Examples: *This students made several mistakes.*

He lived there four year. (years)

She go to school yesterday. (went)

UNIT 8

1. A car owners must have a license.
2. John like science and mathematics.
3. It rains a lot yesterday.
4. Henry is a clever businessmen.
5. Helen reads many magazines, but she doesn't read many book.
6. Her letters is interesting, but it is too short.
7. When Jack drives the car, he sometimes have small accidents.
8. There are five player on a basketball team.
9. English an international language.
10. Although bicycle are small, they are very useful.
11. At this school many boy play football.
12. Thomas A. Edison is born in Ohio in 1847.
13. The child was hurt because he is playing in the street.
14. Plastic materials has many advantages.
15. Story from different countries show us that people everywhere are very much alike.

EXERCISE

F. In Unit 5, page 38, we studied the difference between a sentence and a non-sentence. Below are groups of words, some of which are sentences and some are not. Place an X before each group of words *that is a sentence*. Mark the sentences as quickly as you can, but work carefully.

STRUCTURE EXERCISE

_____ 1. A small child.
_____ 2. A long bus trip.
_____ 3. Both her sons.
_____ 4. Across the street.
_____ 5. He is alone.
_____ 6. A loud noise.
_____ 7. They sang.
_____ 8. Death and destruction.
_____ 9. His brother's return.
_____ 10. The love of money.
_____ 11. The rat died.
_____ 12. Two men in a car.
_____ 13. After the rain.
_____ 14. A new president.
_____ 15. He was worried.
_____ 16. Tired from walking.
_____ 17. All returned safely.
_____ 18. Brave people.
_____ 19. A large place.
_____ 20. The rain stopped.
_____ 21. He loves money.
_____ 22. Surprising news.
_____ 23. A beautiful sunset.
_____ 24. Time goes fast.
_____ 25. Because he was late.

Number correct _____

Now can you explain why those you did not mark are not sentences?

UNIT 8

Answering Questions

G. You have had exercises in which you wrote the answers to questions. In this exercise you will also answer questions, but this exercise is different from those you have done before. Read the paragraph and then follow the directions.

1. Monday was a holiday. I did not go to work. I got up late in the morning and read the newspaper. I went with my family to a restaurant for lunch. We had spaghetti. After that all of us had vanilla ice cream.

    a. Was Monday a holiday?
    b. Did you go to work?
    c. What did you do in the morning?
    d. Where did you go for lunch?
    e. Did you go alone or with your family?
    f. What was the main course for lunch?
    g. What did all of you have for dessert?

Directions: Answer the questions according to the information in the paragraph. Write complete sentences and write them in paragraph form. Do not begin any of your answers with *yes* or *no*.

   Your answers to the first three questions will be exactly the same as the first three sentences in the paragraph. However, your answers to the other questions will be a little different from the sentences in the paragraph. You will have to use your judgment about how to answer the questions correctly.

   When you finish your paragraph, read it carefully to make sure that you have made no mistakes in spelling, punctuation, or grammar. Did you indent the first line of your paragraph?

Spelling

H. 1. Here are some words that were used in these units. You should know the spelling, meaning, and pronunciation of these words.

Nouns
organization — organizations
restaurant — restaurants
magazine — magazines
reco<u>mm</u>endation — reco<u>mm</u>endations
no singular — clothes

Adjectives
busy
tired

NOTICE THE DOUBLE LETTERS

UNIT 8

THIS VERB IS IRREGULAR

Verbs
remember – remembers – remembered
know – knows – knew

Adverb
easily

REVIEW EXERCISE

2. In each of the following groups of words, one word has been misspelled. Write it correctly in the blank space. (Each of the misspelled words has come from the lists of spelling words that you have studied.)

a. meaning, infarmation, useful, clever _____
b. attention, pharmacie, notice, explain _____
c. foriegn, invented, baseball, average _____
d. newspaper, excellent, companny, reader _____
e. topic, handsome, convinient, sentence _____
f. study, desease, general, business _____
g. trafic, seldom, built, different _____
h. alway, belong, supply, imported _____
i. mistakes, finish, dangrous, change _____
j. coffee, necesary, transportation, increase _____

Oral Composition

I. The class will again compose a paragraph orally. The teacher will suggest one of the sentences below as the topic sentence of a paragraph. Students may also suggest topic sentences. The class will choose the topic sentence it prefers. Then the teacher will call on individual students for oral sentences that give additional details about the topic. The details may give various kinds of information.

1. Bicycles provide a simple form of transportation.
2. Electricity is important in our daily lives.
3. Dogs make good pets.

UNIT 8

When a student gives a good oral supporting sentence, he may go to the board and write his sentence after the topic sentence. Each student who gives a good sentence that provides additional information may write his sentence on the board. After the student at the board completes his sentence, other class members may point out any mistakes. Finally, there should be a good paragraph on the board.

When the paragraph is finished, you will make a copy of it to hand in. Be careful about capital letters, punctuation, and spelling.

63

UNIT 9

PARAGRAPH COMPLETION

A. Today you will have a new kind of exercise. The first part of the exercise consists of listening and the second part consists of writing.

The teacher will read a short easy story. Listen to it carefully. At the end of the story, ask questions about any part that you did not understand. The teacher will then read the story a second time, and a third time if you wish. You need to know the story very well. When the reading is finished, the teacher will tell you how to do the written exercise.

SENTENCE LINKS

B. 1. You have learned about several kinds of connections or links between sentences. Here is another common kind of sentence link. Read the examples and notice the underlined words.

Examples:
a. *The auto show is displaying the new cars. These cars have several improvements over last year's models.*

b. *Your space suit will have heavy shoes. These shoes will help you to walk on the moon. The moon does not have as much gravity as the earth does.*

c. *When we read stories from different countries, we see that what is true in one country is also true in another country. These stories show us that people everywhere are very much alike.*

These with a Noun

In the examples the use of these with a noun serves as another kind of sentence link. The word these serves as a pointer. It points back to a word or words used in the preceding sentence.

In example 1, These cars means "the cars that were mentioned in the preceding sentence." In example 2, These shoes means "the shoes that were mentioned in the preceding sentence." The meaning of the third example is similar. The purpose of these is like the purpose of the pronouns he, she, it, etc., in examples given earlier: to avoid repeating the same words. By using these stories the writer avoids saying stories from different countries a second time. If the same words are used too often, the writing becomes monotonous.

The words this, that, and those can be used in the same way as these. Notice how the words are used in the next examples.

64

Examples: d. *The neighborhood consists mostly of apartments, but there is still <u>a large area of one-family houses</u>. <u>That area</u> is where we are making the survey.*

e. *A pottery maker uses <u>a special kind of paint</u>. <u>This paint</u> becomes hard and shiny when the pottery is baked.*

f. *When a person is learning a foreign language, he must learn to recognize <u>new sounds</u>. Then he must learn to make <u>those sounds</u>.*

Summary

2. We have now discussed the use of four kinds of connections or links between sentences:

a. Repeating key words
b. Using personal pronouns (*he, him, she, it,* etc.)
c. Using possessive adjectives (*his, their, my, its,* etc.)
d. Using the words *this, these, that,* and *those* with a noun

EXERCISE

3. In the following selection, underline the words that are the main links between the sentences. Often there are several links between two sentences, but in these sentences underline the links that are similar to the kinds that you have studied so far. Mark each link *a, b, c,* or *d* according to the list above.

Baseball

Baseball is called the national game of the United States. This game has also become popular in several other countries. It is especially popular in Puerto Rico and Japan. Baseball is a summer sport; it is played from early spring until fall.

The best players play for various professional teams. These teams are organized into two major leagues, the National League and the American League. The players are well-known everywhere in the country. They earn big salaries. Their pictures frequently appear in the newspapers.

Millions of sports fans follow the games. They fill baseball parks each year to watch their favorite teams. At other times they watch the games on television or listen to radio broadcasts. Their excitement reaches a peak during the World Series at the end of the season. In this series the top teams of the two major leagues battle for the championship.

UNIT 9

Finding Mistakes in Grammar

C. In Unit 8 you did an exercise in which you corrected the grammar of sentences. Here is another exercise of the same kind. The only difference is that this time the sentences are in a paragraph. Each sentence contains one error in grammar. Correct the sentences.

EXERCISE

The library has many book. The books is about many things. Some books has stories. Other books is about famous men in history. Some famous man in American history are George Washington, Thomas Jefferson, and Abraham Lincoln. There is many books about these men. All American should know about these men. They are important in the history of these country.

D. In the preceding unit you answered questions about a paragraph that was provided for you. This exercise is a little different.

Answer the following questions and write the answers in paragraph form. Do not use the words *yes* or *no.* All answers will be in the affirmative. When you have finished answering the questions, check to make sure of your spelling, punctuation, and grammar. Be especially careful about the verbs. Don't forget to indent the paragraph.

STRUCTURE EXERCISE:
Questions

Example: *Is Helen McGuire a student in our class?*

Helen McGuire is a student in our class.

Did Helen go into the city yesterday? Did she drive her father's new car? Did she go to the dentist? Did she see a dress she liked? Did she buy a blue dress? Did she spend all her money?

E. This exercise is similar to others you have done. You are to write a paragraph beginning with the topic sentence given below and using *some* of the sentences that follow it. Not all of the additional sentences are suitable as supporting sentences. You must decide which sentences are relevant. First read all the sentences. Then follow the directions that come after them.

Assignment:
Relevance

Topic sentence
The development of watches is an interesting story.

Additional sentences
a. A watch is a small timepiece designed to be carried by a person.
b. The first watches were called pocket watches.
c. The first clocks were very large and heavy.

d. It is believed that the first pocket watch was made in Germany in about 1510.
e. The earliest known British clock was put up about 1386.
f. During the sixteenth century watchmaking spread from Germany to England, France, and Switzerland.
g. For a long time English clocks were the most famous in the world.
h. "Big Ben" is a famous clock in London.
i. Wrist watches were first introduced in about 1890.
j. For several years only women wore them, for these "bracelet watches" (as they were called) were considered too feminine for men to wear.
k. The earliest clocks had no dial, but told the hour by striking a bell.
l. However, wrist watches became popular with men during World War I.
m. Since then they have generally been preferred to pocket watches.

Directions: Do this assignment in three steps.
(1) Cross out the sentences that do not support the topic sentence.
(2) Copy the topic sentence and the relevant additional sentences in paragraph form. Copy the sentences in the same order in which they occur.
(3) After you have copied the sentences, read your paragraph and correct any mistakes in spelling, capitalization, or punctuation. Did you indent the first line of the paragraph?

Spelling

F. 1. Here are some words that have been used in these units. You should know their spelling, meaning, and pronunciation.

Nouns
apartment — apartments
friend — friends

NOTICE THE SILENT w.   answer — answers
salary — salaries

THIS NOUN IS IRREGULAR.   woman — women

Adjectives
excellent
special

Verbs
THIS VERB IS IRREGULAR.   come — comes — came
earn — earns — earned

Adverb
again

UNIT 9

REVIEW EXERCISE

2. Some of the words in this list are spelled correctly and some are spelled incorrectly. If the word is correct, write *C* in the blank at the right. If the word is incorrect, write it correctly.

1. beleive _____
2. lose _____
3. bussiness _____
4. probably _____
5. license _____
6. carfully _____
7. convinient _____
8. usualy _____
9. different _____
10. supplys _____
11. dificulty _____
12. opinion _____
13. company _____
14. various _____
15. notise _____
16. weather _____
17. expensive _____
18. acept _____
19. industries _____
20. modren _____

Assignment

G. Study the following paragraph carefully. Your teacher will dictate this paragraph but in a different order. After you finish the dictation, you will have to rearrange the sentences so that they follow each other logically and make sense.

Dictation

Shopping on Saturday is usually difficult. The stores are always crowded. Many people are doing their shopping on the same day. Frequently there are not enough clerks. The clerks are very busy, and late in the day they are tired. In restaurants the service is also slow because there is too much business. For these reasons, some people prefer to shop on other days of the week.

UNIT 10

Dictation

A. The teacher will dictate the paragraph assigned in Unit 9 in the incorrect order. After dictation, rewrite the paragraph, placing the sentences in the correct order.

Review: Choosing Topic Sentences

B. The paragraphs below do not have topic sentences. From sentences *a, b,* or *c,* choose the one that would be the best topic sentence and mark it with an X.

1. In those days people traveled on foot or they rode on horses. Sometimes they rode in wagons or carriages. In 1704 a teacher named Sarah Knight spent seven days traveling from Boston to New York. She rode a horse because the road was too rough for carriages.

    _____ a. People used to travel on horseback or on foot.
    _____ b. People sometimes used to travel in wagons or carriages.
    _____ c. Transportation used to be slow and difficult in the early days of our country.

2. Airlines depend on good weather conditions to keep their planes in the air. Workmen who construct buildings can work only in good weather. Farmers depend on sunshine and rain for growing crops. Merchants find that weather affects their business, for when the weather is bad people do not go shopping.

    _____ a. We should listen to a weather report every day.
    _____ b. Weather is important to a great many people.
    _____ c. Scientists are studying ways to control the weather.

3. It did not snow here in November and December, and there were only a few inches of snow in January and February. In March there wasn't any snow at all. It rained a little in April and May, but in June there were no clouds and it did not rain.

    _____ a. Last year was a dry year in this area.
    _____ b. In January and February there was little snow in this area.
    _____ c. The spring months were very dry last year.

UNIT 10

4. We know that it lies 238,000 miles away. It is about 2,000 miles in diameter, just a quarter the size of the earth. There is no water on the moon. The surface is covered by a layer of ash or dust from four to twelve inches deep. Within a 24-hour period the temperature on the moon's surface may change from 214 degrees above zero to 250 degrees below zero.
   _____ a. The moon is smaller than the earth.
   _____ b. We already know a great deal about the moon.
   _____ c. The moon is lovely to look at from the earth, but it is actually unattractive.

Review: Irrelevant Sentences

C. Each of the following paragraphs has a sentence that is irrelevant. Write the irrelevant sentence on the line below the paragraph.

1. Coin-operated machines have many uses these days. Some of them sell merchandise such as gum, peanuts, candy, cigarettes, and soft drinks. They sometimes get out of order. Some of them provide services; examples of these are washing machines and dry-cleaning machines. Juke boxes are coin machines that play recorded music.
   _____

2. A good weather report tells five things. It predicts what the temperature will be. It tells whether the sky will be cloudy or clear and whether there will be any rain or snow. Most people like clear, sunny weather. A weather report also gives the direction of the wind and the strength of the wind.
   _____

3. In one way or another, nearly all of our food comes from plants. The rice and wheat, the vegetables and the fruit we eat are all forms of plant food. The animal food we eat comes from animals that eat either plants or other animals. These other animals probably eat plants. Some plants need better soil than others.
   _____

4. In Europe during the Middle Ages people used spices to improve the taste of poor food. Spices were more valuable than gold. Today we use spices from all over the world. Black pepper was the most valuable of all the spices. It was used to improve the flavor of meat which was slightly spoiled for lack of refrigeration. This spice was so valuable that sometimes people paid taxes in pepper instead of money.
   _____

UNIT 10

Review: Order of Sentences

D. 1. The following paragraph is not in good order. The sentences should follow time order. Read all the sentences and then write the correct order in which they should appear in the paragraph.

1. She added a cup and a half of water to the mix.
2. She beat everything together in the bowl.
3. Mrs. Jackson emptied the cake mix into a bowl.
4. Mrs. Jackson then poured the batter into two pans and put them into a hot oven.
5. After the water she added two eggs.

Correct order: ____ , ____ , ____ , ____ , ____

2. This paragraph also is not in good order. However, this paragraph does *not* follow time order. First find the sentence that seems to be the topic sentence. Then you can decide on the order of the other sentences by noticing the sentence links.

1. These stories are called folk tales.
2. They do not show us that we are different.
3. Every country has its own stories that people tell each other.
4. Folk tales illustrate something very important about people.
5. Instead they show that people everywhere are very much alike.

Correct order: ____ , ____ , ____ , ____ , ____

Finding Mistakes

E. You have done several exercises in which you added punctuation and capital letters to sentences. In Units 8 and 9 you corrected exercises in which each sentence had an error in grammar. Now you are to correct an exercise which contains two kinds of errors: errors in capitalization and errors in grammar. However, each sentence contains only one error. See how many errors you can find. Make your corrections neatly.

Mother's Day

Mother's Day is day that honors mothers. Several country observe Mother's Day. Among them are England, Sweden, India, and mexico. In the United States the day is observed each year on the second sunday in May. Many people give a gift to their mother on these day. The idea of a special day for mothers was started in this country by Miss Anna Jarvis of philadelphia. The first Mother's Day is held in Philadelphia on May 10, 1908. the

UNIT 10

idea quickly became popular. In 1914 the President of the United States established the second Sunday in may as Mother's Day.

How many capital letters did you put in? _____
How many corrections in grammar did you make? _____

Review:
Subject Pronouns or Possessive Adjectives

F. Fill the blanks with the correct subject pronoun or possessive adjective.

Buster

Charles Davis loves _____ dog Buster. Charles doesn't even mind getting up early in the morning to take Buster for a walk. Charles' wife Betty is not as fond of Buster as _____ husband is. In fact, _____ thinks Buster is a lot of trouble. When Charles is away, for example, Betty has to get up early to take Buster for _____ morning walk. Another thing that annoys Betty is that _____ has to carry so much dog food home from the store. _____ wishes that _____ husband's pet did not have such a large appetite.

Review:
From Questions to Statements

G. This exercise is similar to exercises you have done in previous units. You are to change the questions into statements. Write the statements in the form of a paragraph. Also copy the title of the paragraph.

The Problems of Too Many Cars

Are cars becoming a problem in this country? Do millions of people have cars? Does almost everyone want a car? Does the number of cars increase every year? Does Detroit usually produce more than eight million cars each year? Is traffic a serious problem in every city? Is it difficult to drive during rush hours? Are there many buses and trucks on the streets in addition to passenger cars? Are there more than 100 million motor vehicles in the country? Do these vehicles cause pollution of the air? Is this another serious problem?

UNIT 10

Word Review

H. This exercise will review many of the words in the spelling lists you have had. It will also show how well you can follow directions. Read the directions carefully.

Directions: Do this exercise in four steps:

Step 1. Go through the list and find all the words that are nouns. After each noun, write *N* on the line.
Step 2. Go through the list again and find all the words that are adverbs. After each adverb, write *ADV* on the line.
Step 3. Go through the list again and find all the words that are verbs. Write the *past tense* of the verbs on the line. (You remember that the past tense usually ends in *ed*.)
Step 4. Answer the questions that follow the list.

1. accident _____
2. information _____
3. describe _____
4. usually _____
5. important _____
6. hospital _____
7. explain _____
8. library _____
9. beautiful _____
10. disease _____
11. favorite _____
12. organize _____
13. write _____
14. interesting _____
15. necessary _____
16. always _____
17. successful _____
18. expense _____
19. foreign _____
20. familiar _____
21. busy _____
22. difficult _____
23. company _____
24. opinion _____
25. popular _____
26. convenient _____
27. frequently _____
28. various _____
29. dangerous _____
30. industry _____
31. country _____
32. government _____
33. factory _____
34. business _____
35. different _____
36. contain _____
37. probably _____
38. connection _____
39. restaurant _____
40. clothes _____
41. recommendation _____
42. famous _____
43. know _____
44. finally _____
45. modern _____

73

UNIT 10

Questions:

a. How many words are nouns? _____

b. How many words are adverbs? _____

c. How many words are verbs? _____

d. How many words are not marked? _____

e. What kind of words are the unmarked words? _____

Assignment

I. For this assignment you are to write a composition of your own. In Unit 1 you wrote a paragraph on "What I Did Yesterday." Now you are to write another paragraph on the same subject. Tell what you actually did yesterday. Begin with what you did in the morning and go through the day, following time order. *Remember to use the past tense of verbs.* Also be sure to indent the first line of your paragraph.

    First make a rough draft, then make a neat copy. Finally, read your paragraph carefully to catch any errors you may have made in grammar or punctuation. Also check your spelling. Use the dictionary to look up all the words that you are not completely sure about.

UNIT 11

Paragraph Completion

A. You are to do another exercise in which you complete a paragraph. It is the same kind of exercise that you did in Unit 9. The teacher will read a short easy story and you will listen to it. The teacher will read the story more than once. When the reading is finished, the teacher will give you a written form of the story with several blanks in it. You are to complete the paragraph by filling in the blanks.

LETTER WRITING

B. You will now begin to practice letter writing. Everyone needs to know how to write a letter properly. Letters have a definite form that has to be learned. In addition, various kinds of letters are needed for various purposes, and you should know what kind is suitable for each purpose.

Kinds of Letters

The two main kinds of letters are *business letters* and *personal letters.* Business letters are the kind that you write to a company, to a department of the government, to a school, or to an individual about some business matter. There are many purposes of business letters. You might ask for information, make a request, make a complaint, order merchandise, or apply for a job. Personal letters are the informal, newsy kind that you write to a friend or to a relative.

First you will practice writing business letters. A business letter has six parts: the *heading,* the *inside address,* the *greeting,* the *body,* the *closing,* and the *signature.* Look at the arrangement of the letter on page 76. Find each of the parts.

The Heading

1. The heading consists of your own address and the date on which you are writing. It usually occupies three lines in the upper right corner of the paper.

(Business companies and other organizations use *letterheads* on which their name and address is printed. For this reason they need to type only the date.)

Notice these points about the heading:
a. The first line gives your street address.
b. The second line gives your city, state, and zip code. There

FORM FOR A BUSINESS LETTER

115 Merton Street
New York, NY 10031
March 3, 1972

Jefferson Savings Bank
1172 Broadway
New York, NY 10025

Gentlemen:

    Please send me information about the new savings account plan that you advertised in the <u>Daily News</u>. I am interested in opening an account but would like to receive the booklet that describes the new plan.

Yours truly,
Joseph A. Ferris
Joseph A. Ferris

    should be a comma after the city but not between the state and zip code.

  c. The third line gives the date—first the month, then the day, then the year. There should be a comma between the day and the year.

  d. There should be *no* punctuation at the end of these lines

  e. All three lines should be even on the left side.

  f. The end of the lines should not extend into the margin.

The Inside Address

2. The inside address gives the complete name and address of the person to whom the letter is being sent. The inside address should be the same as the outside address which appears on the envelope. Notice these points:

  a. The address usually has three lines, but it may have four.
    1st line — the name of the person or organization
    2nd line — the street address

UNIT 11

3d line – the city, state, and zip code
4th line – the name of the country (if the letter is going outside the United States)

b. As in the heading, each line should be directly below the line above it, and the lines should be even on the left side.
c. There should be *no* punctuation at the end of these lines.

The Greeting

3. The greeting (also called the *salutation*) consists of the words with which you greet the person or organization to whom you are writing. Notice these points:

a. The greeting is at the left margin, even with the inside address.
b. There is some space between the inside address and the greeting. If you are using a typewriter, leave two spaces.
c. The greeting is followed by a colon (:).
d. The form of greeting depends on whether you are writing to an organization or to a person.
If you are writing to an organization, use *Gentlemen*:
If you are writing to a man, use *Dear Sir* or *Dear Mr.* ——:
If you are writing to a married woman, use *Dear Mrs.* ——:
If you are writing to a single woman, use *Dear Miss* ——:
If you do not know whether a woman is married or single, use *Dear Ms.* ——:

The Body

4. The body of the letter consists of what you are saying to the person or organization. Notice these points:

a. Each paragraph is indented. If you are using a typewriter, indent five spaces.
b. If you are using a typewriter, leave a double space between paragraphs. (The example letter is very brief; many letters have more than one paragraph.)
c. The sentences should be clear and to the point. That means that no words should be wasted in extra statements that do not deal directly with the subject.
d. Although the language should be simple and direct, it should be polite.

The Closing

5. The closing means the words you use to "say goodbye." Notice these points:

a. The closing is placed two spaces (if you are using a typewriter) below the last line of the body of the letter and a little to the right of the center of the page. It should begin directly under the beginning of the heading.

77

b. The closing begins with a capital letter and ends with a comma.
c. Several different expressions may be used for the closing. The usual expressions are:

Yours truly,	Sincerely,
Yours very truly,	Sincerely yours,
Very truly yours,	Yours sincerely,

The Signature

6. Under the closing, sign your name in ink. When using a typewriter, it is customary to type your name also (about four spaces below the closing and directly above the typed signature) so there will be no mistake about the spelling of your name. Notice these points:

a. Use your full name.
b. A man simply signs his name, without *Mr.* or any other title.

John A. Smith

c. A woman signs her name, but under it she should indicate whether she is "Miss" or "Mrs." so that a reply can be addressed to her correctly.

A single woman: *Mary Smith*
(Miss) Mary Smith

A married woman: *Mary Smith*
(Mrs.) Mary Smith

or

Mary Smith
(Mrs. John A. Smith)

Many women, married or single, prefer to use *Ms.*

Appearance of a Business Letter

C. The appearance of a business letter is very important. Remember these points:

1. Write on *white* unlined paper. Write only on one side of the paper. The paper should be regular size; that is, 8½ x 11 inches. (Small sheets are suitable for personal letters, but not for business letters.)
2. Use blue or black ink, never any other color. Never use a pencil for writing a business letter.
3. Leave a margin of at least an inch on the left and on the right. Do not write to the edge of the paper.

UNIT 11

4. As far as possible, center the letter in the middle of the page. The width of the margins depends on the length of the letter. If the letter is short, the margins can be wide. If the letter is long, the margins need to be narrower.
5. The handwriting must be clear and readable.
6. *Be sure* that you have made no mistakes in spelling, grammar, or punctuation.
7. The whole letter should be very neat. There should be no words crossed out or corrections made. If it becomes necessary to make corrections, the letter should be recopied.

EXERCISE

D. Using the information below, write inside addresses and greetings for business letters. The post office recommends the following abbreviations for use with zip codes: IN for Indiana, MI for Michigan, MO for Missouri, NJ for New Jersey, and OH for Ohio.

1. New Jersey 08401   87 Chester Street   Mr. Henry O. Easton   Atlantic City
2. Helen C. Nash   Ohio 45501   Springfield   2021 East 27th Street   Miss
3. Michigan   Steel Products Company   49913   420 Lamont Street   Calumet
4. Director of Research   Indiana   Muncie   Touchstone Laboratories   47302
5. St. Louis   Director of Personnel   501 Western Avenue   63155   Missouri   Ajax Leather Goods, Inc.

Assignment

E. Now you are to write a business letter similar to the example on page 76. Follow carefully the form of the example.

Directions:
1. In the heading, use your own address and the date on which you write the letter.
2. The inside address will be: Madison State Bank, 1307 Porter Street, Baltimore, Maryland 21233. Use a suitable greeting.
3. The body of the letter is given below. You need only to copy it correctly.

   Please send me a new supply of checks. My checking account number is 09-752-133.

4. Use a suitable closing and then sign your own name.

79

UNIT 11

Sentence Links

F. You have studied four ways in which sentences are linked together. How many can you remember? (If you cannot remember all of them, turn back to Unit 9, page 65, and review them.) Now you will become familiar with another common way of linking sentences together.

You know that personal pronouns (*he, she, it,* etc.) are used to avoid repeating the same word. Consequently they are substitutes for other words. There are also other kinds of substitutes, and sometimes they substitute for several words or even an entire sentence. Read the following example and notice the word These. What is These substituting for?

Example 1.   *Several diseases are commonly called children's diseases. These include measles, mumps, chicken pox, and whooping cough.*

You can see that These is substituting for *children's diseases.*
The second sentence could have been written *These diseases include measles, mumps, chicken pox, and whooping cough.* Then it would have been like the sentence links you studied in Unit 9. Here, however, the word These is used alone.

Here is a similar example that uses This:

Example 2.   *Some drivers do not slow down for a red light until the last minute. Then they jam on their brakes and come to a screeching halt. This, of course, is very hard on tires.*

You can see that here This is substituting for almost all of the preceding sentence: *They jam on their brakes and come to a screeching halt.*

What is This substituting for in the next example?

Example 3.   *You may feel sleepy after eating a big dinner. This is because more blood is going to your digestive system and less blood is going to your brain.*

Here you see that This is substituting for the entire preceding sentence: *You may feel sleepy after eating a big dinner.*

G. Each example below has a substitute word underlined. Write what the underlined word is substituting for.

EXERCISE

1.   The children of nomads do not go to school. This creates a problem.

80

UNIT 11

2. People used to believe that the sun went around the earth. They believed this because for many, many years scientists said so.
    _____

3. A helicopter can land and take off in a very small amount of space. This makes it possible to use a helicopter in many places where a large plane cannot go.
    _____

4. If the air becomes cool, the water in the air condenses and finally falls to earth. When this happens, we have rain.
    _____

5. If a farmer grows nothing but cotton, his land will become unproductive and nothing will grow on it. Professor Carver knew this, and he tried to explain it to the farmers.
    _____

6. Checks have advantages over carrying money. If money is lost or stolen, there is little chance of getting it back. A check can be safely mailed. This makes it simple to send money to other parts of the country.
    _____

Assignment

H. You will again write a paragraph by answering some questions. This assignment is similar to one you did in Unit 8. Read the paragraph and then follow directions.

1. June is the month that I like best. The weather is warm, but not hot. In winter the trees are bare and gray, but in June the trees are green. The flowers are bright and pretty. On Saturday and Sunday many people go to the park. They go to see the trees and flowers and to enjoy the fresh air. Most people look happy and relaxed. They wear their light summer clothes. Children run along the walks and visit the animals in the zoo.

Questions

Directions: Answer the questions according to the information in the paragraph. Write complete sentences and write them in paragraph form. Do not begin any of your answers with *yes* or *no*. Some of the answers will be the same or almost the same as the sentences in the paragraph, but some will be different. You will have to use your judgment. Do not use more words than are necessary to answer the question. Not everything in this paragraph will be included in your paragraph, so your paragraph will be a little shorter than this one.

1. Which is your favorite month?
2. How is the weather.
3. How are the trees?
4. How are the flowers?
5. During the weekend what do many people do?
6. Why do they go?
7. How do most people look?
8. Do children go to the park, too?
9. What do they do?

When you finish, count the number of words you have used. You should have no more than 69 words. If you have more, go through the questions again and see if you can shorten your answers. Then write the number of words you have used at the end of the paragraph.

STRUCTURE EXERCISE:
Irregular Verbs

I. 1. It is very important to use irregular verbs correctly. This exercise will help you review some of the common irregular verbs. The present tense is given. Can you give the past tense?

begin	find
bring	forget
buy	get
come	know
do	lose
drink	make
drive	see
eat	write

2. Look at these sentences:
   Mr. Harrison *saw* many interesting things.
   Mrs. Jackson *drank* the hot coffee slowly.
   Alice *told* the story well.

Use the words below to make similar sentences. The first one is done for you.

EXERCISE

a. Mary   buy   a new dress   yesterday

Mary bought a new dress yesterday.

b. Alice Jackson   forget   her history book   yesterday
c. She   bring   it   with her   today

d. Henry Jackson   lose   his math book   last week
e. He   find   it   yesterday
f. Robert Jackson   begin   driving lessons   last week
g. He   drive   his father's car   carefully
h. Mrs. Jackson   make   a chocolate cake   for supper
i. Her children   eat   all the cake
j. They   drink   two quarts of milk   with it
k. Robert   get   very good grades   last semester
l. His teacher   write   nice things   on his report card
m. Robert's father   buy   a cassette player   for him
n. After that   Robert's brother Henry   do   his homework   more often
o. Soon   he   forget   his homework
p. He   see   two movies   last week

Spelling

J. 1. Here are some words that have been used in these units. You should know their spelling, meaning, and pronunciation.

Nouns
a<u>dd</u>ress — a<u>dd</u>resses
ni<u>gh</u>t — ni<u>gh</u>ts
relative — relatives
Saturday — Saturdays

NOTICE THE SILENT LETTERS.

Adjectives
po<u>ss</u>ible
pre<u>tt</u>y
complete

Verbs
ride — rides — rode
reco<u>g</u>nize — reco<u>g</u>nizes — reco<u>g</u>nized

THIS VERB IS IRREGULAR.
NOTICE THE <u>g</u>.

Adverb
of<u>t</u>en

THE <u>t</u> IS SILENT.

Review

2. In each of the following groups of words, one word has been misspelled. Spell it correctly in the blank space. (The misspelled words are from the lists of spelling words that you have studied.)

UNIT 11

a. dificulty, country, finally, experiment _____

b. cheerful, occur, dangerus, probably _____

c. century, unusual, remember, desease _____

d. continue, specail, connect, additional _____

e. include, immediately, organization, neccesary _____

f. beatiful, breathe, careful, visitor _____

g. valley, medcine, repetition, frequently _____

h. foreign, economy, expens, indication _____

i. verious, numerous, previous, attention _____

j. package, climate, perfer, request _____

Assignment

K. Study the following paragraph carefully. Notice the punctuation and capitalization. Be sure you know the spelling of all the words. Be prepared for dictation of this paragraph with several blanks replacing the words. You will be required to fill the blanks with the correct words.

Dictation

More tourists are visiting foreign countries every year. The most popular months for travel are June, July, and August. Tourists are interested in the scenery, the people, and the customs of each country they visit. They are also interested in buying things. They buy articles for themselves. They also buy presents for their relatives and friends. They buy jewelry, perfume, clothes, pictures, and many other things.

UNIT 12

Dictation

A. Do the dictation that was assigned in the preceding unit. The teacher will give you specific directions.

DEPENDENT SENTENCES

B. Notice the underlined word in this sentence:
1. *It* is clean and neat.

This is a correct sentence. When it occurs alone like this, however, you cannot fully understand it. What is clean and neat? Is it a classroom? Is it a boy's shirt? Is it a kitchen? Is it a sidewalk? If you have only this one sentence, you cannot tell what It refers to. To understand the meaning, you must know the sentence or sentences that came before it.

Here are some other examples. Notice the underlined word in each sentence.

Examples:
2. *I am going to buy some flowers for her.*
3. *They will return in ten days.*
4. *The book will help you in another way.*

As you see, each underlined word refers to something that came before. If you do not see the preceding sentences, you cannot understand these sentences. In example 2, who is the person referred to by her? In example 3, who are the people or things referred to by they? In example 4, there is a reference to another way. What other way has been mentioned before? (You have had sentence links like it, her, and they before, but you have not had any like another.)

You cannot understand these sentences unless you see what came before them. Each underlined word is a signal that something necessary to the meaning has appeared in a preceding sentence or preceding sentences.

Now read the examples with the preceding material included, and you will find out what the signals referred to.

1a. *Everyone enjoys visiting Mary's kitchen. It is clean and neat.*
2a. *Our neighbor, Mrs. Smith, is in the hospital. I am going to buy some flowers for her.*

85

UNIT 12

3a. *Mr. and Mrs. Martinez left yesterday for a trip to Puerto Rico. <u>They</u> will return in ten days.*

4a. *This chemistry book will help you because it is written in a clear and simple way. The book will help you in <u>another</u> way. In the back there is a list of words often used in chemistry.*

You can see from the examples that a sentence that contains links like these is not understandable when it is alone. It is *dependent* upon another sentence in the paragraph for a complete understanding of its meaning. Each sentence with such linking words fits into a paragraph in a certain way. This is why sentences usually must follow each other in a certain order. This is the reason why we have been studying sentence links.

EXERCISE

C. The following sentences are similar to the examples. Underline the words that show that these sentences are dependent upon preceding sentences. We have not discussed most of these words, but see if you can choose them by yourself.

1. The teacher considered her a very good student.
2. He did many different kinds of work.
3. The space suit will also have heavy shoes.
4. A lot of cotton is grown in other parts of the United States.
5. But cotton takes chemicals from the soil.
6. Consequently a serious problem had to be solved.
7. The scientist tried an additional experiment.
8. This time the French team won the game.
9. Their ideas about education have changed.
10. Later the styles changed and skirts became very short.
11. The experiment showed, however, that the idea was possible.
12. Finally the teacher pointed out the answer to the problem.
13. In some years, for example, grapes are poor because of bad weather.
14. The man still could not reach his hat in the river.
15. Then they spent an hour eating lunch.

Notice that the last sentence has *two* words that should be underlined.

Important Points

D. There are two important things to remember about sentences like those in B and C:

UNIT 12

1. A sentence may be complete and *independent* as far as grammar is concerned, but it may be *dependent* as far as its position in the paragraph is concerned.

2. A dependent sentence usually cannot be used as the first sentence in a paragraph. The first sentence should be independent.

STRUCTURE EXERCISE

E. 1. There are several blank spaces in the paragraph below. You are to decide what *kind* of word (noun, verb, or adjective) belongs in each blank space. Then write the kind of word *under* each blank.

Example: *It was a* _____ *day.*
                    adjective

Saturday was a _____ day. I took a _____
                         1   2
walk. First I _____ to a park that is near my house. For a while
                      3
I watched a softball game. Then I _____ from the park to my
                                                          4
cousin's house. It was a very long walk. I sat and _____ with him
                                                                              5
for a while. From his house I_____ to a clothing_____.
                                              6   7
I looked at jackets and_____. I did not buy anything because
                                      8
everything was_____. By that time I was _____.
                              9   10
I came home on a _____. It_____ six o'clock.
                                11   12

2. After you have written the kinds of words under the lines, go back and see how many blanks you can fill with suitable words. Write these words *above* the lines.

LETTER WRITING

Addressing the Envelope

F. 1. In the preceding unit you began to practice letter writing. You also need to know how to address the envelope.

The envelope of the letter to the Jefferson Savings Bank (the example letter in Unit 11) would look like this.

UNIT 12

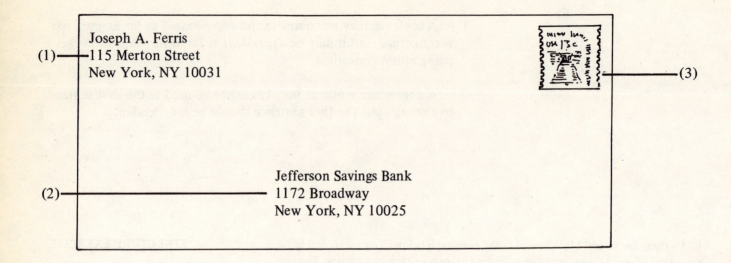

Here are some points to notice about the envelope.

(1) The person who sends the letter puts his name and address in the upper left corner of the envelope. This is called the *return address*. This means that if the letter cannot be delivered for some reason, it will be returned to the sender. This address is the same as the address in the heading of the letter.

(2) The name and address of the company or person who is to receive the letter should go in the center of the envelope. It is exactly the same as the inside address of the letter.
   If you are sending the letter to a person instead of a company, the points to remember are these:
   a. The person's full name goes on the first line.
   b. The person's name should be preceded by some kind of title, depending on whether the person is a man, an unmarried woman, or a married woman.

   Man: Mr. James Pearson *or* Mr. James H. Pearson
   Unmarried
      woman: Miss Helen Pearson *or* Ms. Helen Pearson
   Married
      woman: Mrs. James Pearson *or* Mrs. Martha Pearson
               or Ms. Martha Pearson

   c. Notice that there is a period after *Mr., Mrs.,* and *Ms.* They are abbreviations.

(3) The stamp or stamps should go in the upper right corner of the envelope.

UNIT 12

EXERCISE

2. On a piece of paper draw four oblongs to look like envelopes. They should look like the example envelope on page 88. On each "envelope" write your own address (the return address) in the upper left corner. Then address the four envelopes, using this information for the addresses:

a. 44101   Annabelle Colton   Ohio   Miss   Cleveland   192 Crestview Street

b. Harold Barr   Houston   1800 Leland Avenue   77002   Mr.   Texas (TX)

c. 16 Asbury Street   Elwin Robertson   New Jersey   Mrs.   Plainfield   07061

d. Miami   38 Merrill Drive   Sterling Travel Service   33101   Florida (FL)

Folding a Letter

3. There is a definite form for folding a letter. The way it is folded depends on the size of the envelope. Your teacher will show you how a letter should be folded to fit a small envelope and a large envelope.

STRUCTURE EXERCISE

G. As you know, the verb should agree with the subject of a sentence. If the subject is singular, the verb should be singular. If the subject is plural, the verb should be plural. In some of the sentences that follow, the verb does not agree with the subject. If the verb agrees, write C (for Correct) on the line. If the verb does not agree, cross out the verb in the sentence and write it correctly on the line.

Examples: *The bus leaves on time every morning.*   ___C___

The boys ~~plays~~ football every afternoon.   ___play___

1. Stores are busy on Saturday.   _____

2. Many people is in the stores.   _____

3. My friends shops at a shopping center.   _____

4. Joseph go to school every day.   _____

5. The children next door go to school with Joseph.   _____

UNIT 12

6. Harry often watch baseball on TV. _____
7. He like baseball very much. _____
8. Mr. Jackson takes his lunch to work. _____
9. He work for a large company. _____
10. Mr. Jackson and Mr. Williams work at the same palce. _____
11. They likes their jobs. _____
12. They often get overtime pay. _____
13. The extra salary helps with their bills. _____
14. The cost of living is high these days. _____
15. The price of groceries increase all the time. _____

Finding Mistakes

H. In this exercise there are two kinds of errors—errors in capitalization and in grammar. However, there is only one error in each sentence. Can you find the errors? Make your corrections neatly.

Washington

Washington is the capital of the united states. It are the center of our national government. The President live in the White House. The city was named for george washington. She was the first President of the country. There are many government office in Washington. there are not many factory there. Washington was a beautiful city. The weather is often very hot on summer.

How many capital letters did you put in? _____
How many changes did you make in grammar? _____

Assignment: Answering Questions

I. 1. You have done several exercises in which you wrote paragraphs by changing a series of questions into statements. Here is another exercise in which you answer questions, but this exercise is different from those you have done before. In this exercise you are to give your own answers to the questions. You will do this exercise in class. If you do not know how to answer some of the questions, the teacher will help you.

Be careful about the tense of your verbs. One purpose of this assignment is to give you more practice in writing the past tense.

Sunday

Did you enjoy your day off on Sunday? Did you sleep late in the morning? When you got up, did you eat a large breakfast? Did you read the Sunday paper? Did you go to church? In the afternoon, did you go window-shopping? Did you go alone or did you go with (family members, friends)? Later did you (singular or plural) decide to see a movie? Was it a good movie or a poor movie? Did you return home in time for supper? After supper did you watch TV? How long did you watch TV? What time did you go to bed?

2. When you finish your paragraph, the teacher will check it. Then make a neat copy of it. After you have copied it, *be sure to copyread it before you hand it in.*

STRUCTURE EXERCISE: Complete and Incomplete Sentences

J. 1. Some of the groups of words below are sentences, but some are not. Place an X before each group of words *that is a sentence.* The sentence may be a statement or an order or request (imperative). Work quickly but carefully.

_____ 1. Two and two make four.
_____ 2. A long, hot summer.
_____ 3. The voice of the teacher.
_____ 4. Trees and their branches.
_____ 5. Progress is slow.
_____ 6. A beautiful cat.
_____ 7. Listen carefully.
_____ 8. Too much sunshine.
_____ 9. Dark sunglasses.
_____ 10. Over the radio.
_____ 11. They spoke loudly.
_____ 12. A bad cold.
_____ 13. The tan overcoat.
_____ 14. In the kitchen.
_____ 15. The sound of birds.
_____ 16. A pen in his hand.
_____ 17. The small chair broke.
_____ 18. Horses are animals.
_____ 19. The middle of the road.
_____ 20. A small broken chair.
_____ 21. Military airplanes.
_____ 22. He dropped the pen.
_____ 23. Holding a green umbrella.
_____ 24. Textbooks on grammar.
_____ 25. Accidents occur frequently.
_____ 26. Half an apple.
_____ 27. Because it rained.
_____ 28. A small piece of chalk.
_____ 29. Reading the newspaper.
_____ 30. I need a book.

Number correct _____

UNIT 12

2. Now can you explain why the groups of words you did not mark are not sentences?

Spelling

K. 1. Here are some words that have been used in these units. You should know their spelling, meaning, and pronunciation.

Nouns
article — articles

NOTICE THAT <u>gh</u> IS SILENT. nei<u>gh</u>bor — nei<u>gh</u>bors
appea<u>r</u>ance — appea<u>r</u>ances
merchandise — *no plural*

NOTICE THE <u>r</u> AFTER <u>b</u>. Fe<u>br</u>uary — *plural seldom used*

Adjectives

NOTICE THAT <u>gh</u> SOUNDS LIKE <u>f</u>. enou<u>gh</u>
im<u>p</u>ossible

Verbs
a<u>p</u>ply — a<u>p</u>plies — a<u>p</u>plied

NOTICE THE SILENT <u>p</u>. em<u>p</u>ty — em<u>p</u>ties — em<u>p</u>tied

Adverb
already

Words Ending in y

2. You have practiced the spelling of words that end in *y*. When *y* is preceded by a consonant, how do you form the plural? Can you give examples?

The *y* words you have had so far in spelling lists have been nouns. There are also verbs that end in a consonant and *y*. You have two of them in today's spelling list (*apply* and *empty*). As you see, these verbs have an *s* form (the third person singular) that is made in the same way as the plural of nouns.

Here are some more verbs. How would you write the *s* form?

a. cry _____   d. study _____

b. try _____   e. copy _____

c. fly _____   f. deny _____

Both nouns and verbs have an *s* form, but in nouns the *s* form is the plural and in verbs the *s* form is the third person singular. Perhaps

UNIT 12

the easiest way to remember the rule is to change Spelling Rule (1) so that it covers both nouns and verbs:

Spelling Rule (1a)   If a word ends in *y* preceded by a consonant, make the *s* form by changing *y* to *i* and adding *es*.

Alphabetical Order

L. When you use a telephone directory, a dictionary, a filing system, or a library, you need to be familiar with alphabetical order.

1. Copy these words in alphabetical order.

EXERCISE

lose	buy	famous	telephone
country	produce	accident	easily
know	difficult	magazine	weather

(1) _____   (7) _____
(2) _____   (8) _____
(3) _____   (9) _____
(4) _____   (10) _____
(5) _____   (11) _____
(6) _____   (12) _____

2. When you have several words that begin with the same letter, you arrange them alphabetically according to the second letter of each word. Copy these words in alphabetical order.

EXERCISE

| grow | glad | gallon | gum | gymnasium |
| girl | germ | ghost | gold | gem |

(1) _____   (6) _____
(2) _____   (7) _____
(3) _____   (8) _____
(4) _____   (9) _____
(5) _____   (10) _____

UNIT 13

Paragraph Completion

A. Here is another exercise in which you complete a paragraph. You are now familiar with this kind of exercise. The teacher will read a short, easy story and you will listen to it. The teacher will read the story more than once. When the reading is finished, you will receive a written form of the story with several blanks in it. You are to complete the paragraph by filling in the blanks.

IDENTIFYING TOPIC SENTENCES

B. You have had exercises in which you choose suitable topic sentences for paragraphs. This exercise is a little different. Some of the paragraphs have topic sentences, but some do not. You are to decide which paragraphs have topic sentences. Mark those paragraphs with an X.

_____ 1. The stores are crowded because most people do not work on this day. Often there are not enough clerks. A person often has to wait a long time to get waited on. The service in restaurants is also slow on Saturday.

_____ 2. Our holiday was very enjoyable. Our club went on a picnic. We went to a beautiful park about ten miles from the city. It was very cool and pleasant in the shade of the trees. We spent the afternoon eating, talking, and playing football.

_____ 3. There is a large choice of food and the students can fill their trays quickly. There are enough tables and chairs and they are not too close together. The lighting is good. The walls are painted a cheerful color. Even when there are many students there, the room is not very noisy.

_____ 4. The game was the most exciting one of the season. It was the last game of the series and each side wanted very much to win. Because the players were nervous, they made many mistakes. First one team would get ahead and then the other. The spectators were noisy. Every time a player made a basket, the crowd roared.

_____ 5. People vote for candidates for various reasons. Some people vote for a candidate because he favors policies that will benefit them personally. Some people vote for a candidate because they like his looks and personality, or they dislike his opponent's looks and personality. Some people vote for a man simply because he is the candidate of their party.

_____ 6. TV and radio advertisements urge us to buy certain kinds of detergent, furniture polish, coffee, toothpaste, or headache tablets. Newspaper and magazine advertisements tell us to buy certain kinds of cars, refrigerators, and clothing. Billboard ads praise certain kinds of gasoline, motor oil, or cigarettes. In the mail we receive ads for many other products.

"Scrambled" Paragraphs

C. In this exercise you will again arrange sentences in good order to make coherent paragraphs. You are to number the sentences in the order in which they should come in the paragraphs. Follow the directions.

Directions. Do the exercise in these steps:
(1) Read all the sentences in a group and choose the one that is best suited for the topic sentence. Mark this *1*.
(2) Look for signals (sentence links) that show you how the other sentences fit together. Write the correct order for the sentences on the lines provided.
(3) Underline the signals.

EXERCISE

1.
   1. Doctors give it to people who have an infection of some kind.
   2. It has saved many lives since it was discovered.
   3. They also give it to persons who have been hurt in an accident.
   4. Penicillin was discovered about forty-five years ago. ____, ____, ____, ____

2.
   1. Migrant workers are people who move from place to place.
   2. Consequently the children do not learn to read or write.
   3. Their children do not go to school.
   4. They take their families and possessions with them. ____, ____, ____, ____

UNIT 13

3.
1. Then she could not find a position
2. Later she established a medical college for women.
3. Elizabeth Blackwell was the first woman doctor in the United States.
4. After trying for three years to find a position, she established her own hospital.
5. She had a great deal of difficulty getting a medical education because she was a woman.

_____ , _____ , _____ , _____ , _____

D. Copy the paragraphs in section C, arranging the sentences in which you numbered them. Copyread your paragraphs before you hand in your paper.

Assignment

E. 1. The word *but* is often used to join two sentences and make one sentence. Look at these two sentences:

I know George.   I don't know Paul.

Here the second sentence expresses something that is the opposite of the thought in the first sentence. If you want to put these two thoughts together into one sentence, you can do it like this:

I know George, but I don't know Paul.

The word *but* joins the two ideas and it also does something else: it shows that the two ideas are different from each other. That is, they *contrast* with each other.

STRUCTURE EXERCISE

2. How would you use contrasting ideas in these sentences? Fill in the blanks.

a. Winter is cold. Summer is _____?

b. John is fat. Henry is _____.

c. A bicycle is small. An airplane is _____.

d. This radio is expensive. That radio is _____.

e. My brother is noisy. My sister is _____.

f. Bill's car is new. Don's car is _____.

Now that you have filled in the blanks, combine the sentences into one sentence by using *but*. The first one is done for you.

a. *Winter is cold, but summer is hot.*

3. Can you think of sentences similar to those in 2? See if you can think of one or two similar sentences of your own. Say them when the teacher calls on you.

EXERCISE

UNIT 13

EXERCISE

4. Write the following sentences by combining them into one sentence with *but*. Use a comma before the word *but*.

a. I know Ray. I don't know Ray's wife.
b. Evelyn likes English. She doesn't like math.
c. Joe likes cake with frosting. He doesn't like plain cake.
d. Richard reads magazines. He doesn't read books.
e. Elizabeth reads fashion magazines. She doesn't read other magazines.
f. The first movie wasn't interesting. The second movie was good.
g. The game yesterday was exciting. The game today is dull.
h. My last car was bad. The one I have now is good.
i. Hazel's dress is pretty. It is too short.
j. The stories in this book are interesting. The vocabulary is difficult.

Assignment:
Relevance and Coherence

F. You are to write a paragraph beginning with the topic sentence given and using some of the additional sentences. You must decide which of the additional sentences are irrelevant. Read all the sentences and then follow the directions.

Topic sentence:
   The history of banking is very old.

Additional sentences:
1. Ancient writers mentioned money changers and money lenders.
2. This is where the word *bank* comes from.
3. Modern banks provide many services to their customers.
4. The first real bank was established in Venice, Italy.
5. The Italian word for bench is *banco*.
6. Other Italian cities started banks.
7. A check is a safe and convenient way to carry money.
8. Slowly banking activities spread from Italy to other places in Europe.
9. Centuries ago the merchants of Italy were well-known money changers.
10. These money changers often conducted their business on benches in the market place.   ____, ____, ____, ____, ____, ____, ____, ____, ____, ____

Directions. Do this exercise in these steps:
(1) Cross out the sentences that do not support the topic sentence.
(2) Sentence 1 should follow the topic sentence, but the remaining sentences are not in good order. Rearrange them so as to form a good paragraph. The signals (sentence links) will help you to fit the sentences together in good order. Write the correct order on the lines provided.
(3) When you have the relevant sentences in good order, copy the topic sentence and the supporting sentences in paragraph form.
(4) Copyread the paragraph before you hand it in.

Spelling

G. 1. Here is one more rule for spelling words that end in *y*. You know how to make the *s* form when a word ends in a consonant and

97

UNIT 13

y. What happens when a word ends in a vowel and *y*? You simply add *s*.

Examples: *alley – alleys   (noun)*
enjoy – enjoys   (verb)

Spelling Rule (2)

When a word ends in *y* preceded by a vowel, make the *s* form by adding *s*.

Now write the *s* form of these words:

a. company _____   d. study _____

b. valley _____   e. difficulty _____

c. pay _____   f. obey _____

Review

2. Each of the following sentences contains a word that is not spelled correctly. The misspelled words are from spelling lists that you have studied. Correct each misspelled word.

Examples: *Education is one of the main activities of the goverment.*   government
He is very populer with his classmates.   popular

a. Dave likes his job, but he does not earrn enough money.
b. A frend told Dave about a job in another company.
c. That job has a better salery than Dave's present job.
d. It seems like an intresting job.
e. The work is similiar to his present work.
f. The job is with a large business organzation.
g. Dave applyed for the job last week.
h. He is now waiting for an anser to his application.
i. Dave hopes that his present boss will give him a good reccomendation.
j. Of course he hopes that he will be sucessful in getting the job.

Words to Know

3. Here are some words that have been used in these units. You should know their spelling, meaning, and pronunciation.

Nouns
trouble – troubles
application – applications
envelope – envelopes
child – children

THIS NOUN IS IRREGULAR.

98

UNIT 13

Adjectives
definite
cert<u>ai</u>n

COMPARE THIS WITH <u>believe</u>.

Verbs
rec<u>ei</u>ve — rec<u>ei</u>ves — rec<u>ei</u>ved
<u>app</u>ear — <u>app</u>ears — <u>app</u>eared
decide — decides — decided

NOTICE THE SECOND <u>e</u>.

Adverb
since<u>re</u>ly

Words Often Confused: there/their

H. The words *there* and *their* are sometimes confusing. The two words have the same pronunciation but different meanings. To find out how well you can use these words, fill in the blanks in these sentences.

1. Some of the students were unhappy when they received _____ grades.

2. The Johnsons moved into _____ new apartment last month.

3. If you intend to visit the Johnsons, you had better find out _____ new address.

4. It will take you about thirty minutes to get _____ on the bus.

5. I wanted to call the Johnsons, but I didn't know _____ new telephone number.

6. This letter is going to San Francisco. How long will it take for it get _____ ?

7. I have lost my English book. I had it when I went to the cafeteria for a coke. I must have left it _____.

8. The office manager pointed to a place over by the window and said to the moving men, "Put the desk over _____.

9. Ted and Nick are brothers. Both of them brought home excellent report cards from school last month. _____ parents are proud of them.

99

UNIT 13

10. I telephoned Mr. and Mrs. Lopez last evening to congratulate them on _____ wedding anniversary.

Oral Composition

I. The class will again compose a paragraph orally. The teacher will write on the chalkboard one of the sentences below to be chosen by the students as the topic sentence of a paragraph. Then the teacher will call on individual students for oral sentences that give additional details about the topic.

Topic sentences:
1. Owning a car is expensive.
2. The cost of living continues to rise.
3. Living in a city involves problems.

When a student gives a good oral supporting sentence, he may go to the board and write his sentence following the topic sentence. Each student who gives a good sentence that provides additional information may write his sentence on the board.

After the student at the board completes his sentence, other class members may point out any mistakes he has made in grammar, spelling, or punctuation. Finally, there should be a good paragraph on the board. When it is finished, each student should make a copy of it to hand in.

Assignment

J. Study the following paragraph. Notice the punctuation; there are numerous commas in this selection. Be sure you know the spelling of all the words. Be ready for dictation of this paragraph.

Writing Letters

Everyone should know how to write a letter properly. Letters have a definite form that must be learned. The two main kinds of letters are business letters and personal letters. Business letters are the kind that you write to a company, to a department of the government, to a school, or to an individual about some business matter. Business letters have various purposes. You might ask for information, make a request, make a complaint, order merchandise, or apply for a job. Personal letters are the kind that you write to a friend or a relative.

UNIT 14

Dictation

A. Do the dictation that was assigned in the preceding unit.

Choosing Supporting Details

B. You have had practice in choosing topic sentences. Now this exercise will give you practice in noticing supporting details.

Look at the first example. You are familiar with this paragraph. The first sentence is the topic sentence and the sentences that follow are supporting sentences. On the blank lines are the main points of the supporting sentences.

Example 1.   *John is a very good student. He does his homework every night. His notebook is neat. He is always able to answer correctly when the teacher calls on him. He usually gets A on his examinations.*

    does homework every night
    notebook is neat
    answers correctly
    gets A on exams

Now look at the next example. Read the paragraph and then write the *main points* of the supporting sentences. You need not write complete sentences.

Example 2.   *Because of changes made by science, the world today is very different than it was a hundred years ago. Now we can fly across oceans. We can talk to people thousands of miles away. We can have light instantly whenever we need it. We can get medicine for most diseases.*

_____
_____
_____
_____

101

UNIT 14

C. Now read the next paragraphs and follow the same procedure. The purpose of this exercise is to see if you can find the most important points that a writer uses to support his topic sentence.

EXERCISE

1. Owners of small cars believe that these cars have advantages over large ones. A small car is inexpensive to operate because it goes 20 to 30 miles on a gallon of gasoline. The original purchase price of a small car is considerably less than that of the bigger models. And of course small cars are much easier to park.

   _____
   _____
   _____

2. Most Americans would benefit by doing more walking. Doctors say that walking is one of the best forms of exercise. In good weather, a walk is a pleasant form of recreation. When you are feeling lonely or depressed, a long walk can do a lot to cheer you up.

   _____
   _____
   _____

3. Since the early days of airplanes, many improvements have been made in their construction. Because of better instruments, planes can now fly safely at night and in bad weather. Because of their increased size, they can carry a very large number of passengers. Probably the greatest improvement in air transportation has been the jet engine, which makes flying very fast.

   _____
   _____
   _____

Writing Topic Sentences

D. In exercise C you identified supporting details. In this exercise you are given supporting details which need a topic sentence. See if you can write suitable topic sentences. First decide on the topic of the paragraph and then make a statement about it.

EXERCISE

1. _____

Some people like rainy weather because they are allergic to dust. Some people prefer dry weather because dampness is bad for their health. Other people like hot summer weather because they are uncomfortable when it is cold.

2. _____

She cleaned all the rugs with the vacuum cleaner. She dusted all the furniture. She cleaned the bathroom. In the kitchen she cleaned the stove and mopped the floor. Then Mrs. Morales began to make a cake to have for dinner on Sunday.

3. _____

He colors the walls with his crayons. He breaks the toys I give him to play with. He spills food on the carpet and makes marks on the furniture with his sticky fingers. In fact, I dread a visit from my brother's little boy.

Copyreading

E. In the following sentences there are two kinds of errors—errors in spelling and errors in grammar. However, each sentence has only one error. Can you find the errors? Make your corrections neatly.

1. Yesterday I write several letters.
2. One letter was an aplication letter.
3. I copied it carefully because the appearance of a business letter is important.
4. Two of my letters was personal letters.
5. First I write to my friend Linda.
6. I sent her a letter in Febuary, but I did not receive an answer.
7. I decided to write to her agian.
8. Linda is having a lot of trouble this year.

103

UNIT 14

9. Her husband have been sick.
10. My second personal letter was to a relativ, my Uncle George.
11. I have two uncle, George and Henry.
12. My Uncle George lives in New Jersey and my Uncle Henry live in California.
13. My Uncle George has two childern.
14. My uncles is very kind men.
15. I am going to visit my Uncle George next Saterday.

How many misspelled words did you correct? _____

How many mistakes in grammar did you correct? _____

Letter Writing: Abbreviations

F. Here are some additional points to remember about business letters.

1. The titles *Mr., Mrs.,* and *Ms.* are always followed by a period. This is because they are abbreviations. *Miss* is not followed by a period because it is a complete word.

2. Another common title is *Dr.* (the abbreviation of *Doctor*). Because it is an abbreviation, it should always be used with a period.

3. Some words similar to *street* are: *avenue, boulevard, road, drive.* Sometimes these words are abbreviated: *ave., blvd., rd., dr.* In our letter-writing practice, however, you should write them out in full.

4. Sometimes, as with zip codes, the names of states are abbreviated, but at this stage of practice you should write them out in full. There will be two exceptions:
   New York, New York. Write: *New York, N.Y.* or *New York, NY*
   Washington, District of Columbia. Write: *Washington, D.C.* or *Washington, DC.*

These names of places will be abbreviated because that is the way they are commonly used.

Punctuation

G. You now know another rule for punctuation:

Punctuation Rule (3): The Period   Use a period after most abbreviations.

UNIT 14

Notice that the rule does not say after *all* abbreviations. Some abbreviations are commonly used without periods; examples are *exam, gym, UN, TV, FBI*. You will have to learn as you go along which ones need periods and which do not.

Assignment: Letter Writing

H. You will again practice business letter writing. This time you are to order a publication. Everyone occasionally spills something, such as coffee, juice, grease, or paint, on his or her clothing. For this reason it is convenient for a household to have on hand a booklet that explains how to remove stains from clothing. The United States Government Printing Office in Washington is a source of information.

(It is useful to know about this office, since it issues publications on thousands of different subjects. The publications are not all free, but the charge is usually small.)

The inside address and the body of your letter are given. You are to supply the other parts of the letter.

Inside Address
Superintendent of Documents
U. S. Government Printing Office
Washington, D.C. 20402

(The abbreviation *U. S.* is used here because this is the way the Printing Office writes its name.)

Body of the letter
Please send me Home Bulletin No. 62, "Removing Stains from Fabrics." I enclose 15 cents.

(Notice that the title of the publication has quotation marks at the beginning and end.)

STRUCTURE EXERCISE:
Complete and Incomplete Sentences

I. 1. This exercise is similar to ones you have done before. Some of the groups of words below are sentences, but some are not. Place an X before each group of words that is *not* a sentence. Work quickly but carefully.

_____ 1. Received an important letter.

_____ 2. Unusually cold weather.

_____ 3. Ancient people discovered it.

_____ 4. Numerous accidents on the road.

_____ 5. Oriental rugs are famous.

_____ 6. Lost a valuable watch.

_____ 7. Broken dishes.

_____ 8. This is a difficult problem.

_____ 9. A sudden loud cry.

UNIT 14

_____ 10. He fell down suddenly.
_____ 11. A truck loaded with merchandise.
_____ 12. Several reasons for the increase in tourists.
_____ 13. An especially interesting story.
_____ 14. He used a dictionary.
_____ 15. A sweater is needed during this season.
_____ 16. Attends a movie occasionally.
_____ 17. Did not recognize the person.
_____ 18. Science important in the modern world.
_____ 19. Looks like the photograph.
_____ 20. She appreciated the present.
_____ 21. Because it was very late.
_____ 22. After coming home from the party.
_____ 23. All the people believed it.
_____ 24. A letter to a friend in another city.
_____ 25. The people were living in the country.
_____ 26. Contains useful information.
_____ 27. The best workers in the group.
_____ 28. All the doctors in the hospital.
_____ 29. When the police arrived.
_____ 30. Because it was the shortest road.

Number correct _____

2. Now can you explain why those you marked are not sentences?

J. This exercise is similar to one you did in Unit 11. You are to make sentences from the vocabulary given below. This time you will practice sentences that use the word *but*.

STRUCTURE EXERCISE:
Sentences using *but*

Examples: *Arthur   be   small   be   strong*
<u>*Arthur is small, but he is strong.*</u>

Evelyn   like   English   do not   like   math
<u>*Evelyn likes English, but she does not like math.*</u>

Look at the examples carefully. Notice the changes that have been made in the underlined sentences. Now do the exercise, using the words to make similar sentences.

1. Maria   speak   Spanish   do not   speak   English
2. She   study   English   do not   use   it
3. Charles   study   math   do not   enjoy   it
4. The winters here   be   cold   summers   be   hot

106

5. Charles watch TV a lot do not study math
6. He enjoy TV movies do not enjoy commercials
7. Betty receive letters do not answer them
8. The days be hot nights be cool
9. My wife often bake cakes do not bake pies
10. Paul do not buy movie tickets buy lottery tickets
11. Cars be useful they be expensive
12. Carl drive his father's car do not buy gas for it
13. Madeline like sewing Gloria prefer knitting
14. Jackie like baseball Ted prefer football
15. Henry enjoy Western movies Ben do not like them

Assignment

K. This assignment is similar to those you did in Units 8 and 11. Read the paragraph and then follow directions.

Sunday

Sunday was a fine October day. The day was unusually warm for this time of year. We went to the park in the afternoon because the weather was so lovely. We walked along the paths to see the fall flowers. They were still beautiful. The trees were very colorful. The sun shone brightly on their yellow, red, brown, and tan leaves.

Directions. Answer the questions according to the information in the paragraph. Write complete sentences and write them in paragraph form. Do not begin any of your answers with *yes* or *no*. Some of the answers should be the same or almost the same as the sentences in the paragraph, but some should be different. You will have to use your judgment. Do not use more words in your answer than are necessary to answer the question. Not everything in this paragraph will be included in your paragraph, so your paragraph will be shorter than this one.

1. Was Sunday a fine October day?
2. Where did you (plural) go in the afternoon?
3. Why did you go?
4. Where did you walk?
5. Why did you walk there?
6. How were the fall flowers?
7. Were the trees drab or colorful?
8. What colors were the leaves?
   (Do not use the word *colors* in your answer. Begin your answer: "The leaves were . . . . .")

When you finish, count the number of words you have used. You should have no more than 52 words. If you have more than this, go through the questions again to see if you can shorten your answers. Write the number of words you have used at the end of your paragraph.

Finally, copyread your paragraph.

UNIT 14

Alphabetical Order: Review

L. 1. Number the following words according to the order they would have if they were arranged alphabetically. No. 1 is done for you.

_____ come	__1__ apartment	_____ article
_____ believe	_____ describe	_____ usually
_____ organize	_____ government	_____ interesting
_____ sincerely	_____ disease	_____ know
_____ neighbor	_____ possible	_____ merchandise

2. The first two letters of the following words are the same. How would you arrange the words in alphabetical order?

| floor | flat | flew | flunk | fly |
| flash | flower | flag | flight | flip |

(1) _____ (6) _____

(2) _____ (7) _____

(3) _____ (8) _____

(4) _____ (9) _____

(5) _____ (10) _____

Spelling: *ie* and *ei* words

M. 1. Look at these words, which you have had in spelling lists or in exercises:

believe	foreign
receive	friend
neighbor	their

Notice that in some of these words the *i* comes before the *e,* and in some of them the *e* comes before the *i*. How can you remember the correct spelling? The best way is to memorize the new *ie* and *ei* words as you meet them in spelling lists or in exercises, and then review them frequently.

There is one rule that will help you, although there are exceptions:

Spelling Rule (3)

In syllables with an *ee* sound (as in *need*), *i* comes before *e* except after *c*.

Examples: *bel<u>ie</u>ve   rec<u>ei</u>ve*
               p<u>ie</u>ce   dec<u>ei</u>ve
               f<u>ie</u>ld   c<u>ei</u>ling

What about the word *neighbor*? It does not have the *ee* sound; instead it is pronounced like *nayber*. Another word pronounced like this is *weigh* (pronounced the same as *way*). Notice that in these words the *e* is also before the *i*. Perhaps you can remember this if you learn a little rhyme:

Put *i* before *e*,
Except after *c*,
Or when sounded like *a*,
As in *neighbor* and *weigh*.

What about the words *friend, foreign,* and *their*? These words are not pronounced like *ee* or like *ay*. They are special cases and probably the best thing to do is simply to memorize their spelling.

EXERCISE

2. How would you spell the following words? All are pronounced with the *ee* sound (the sound in *need*).

a. n _ _ ce
b. pr _ _ st
c. th _ _ f
d. conc _ _ ted
e. ch _ _ f
f. perc _ _ ve

Words to Know

3. Here are some words that have been used in these units. You should know their meaning, pronunciation, and spelling.

Nouns
advertisement — advertisements
material — materials
account — accounts

UNIT 14

Adjectives
com**mon**
pleasant
valuable

Verbs
THIS VERB IS IRREGULAR. break — breaks — broke
advertise — advertises — advertised
appreciate — appreciates — appreciated

Adverb
sometimes

Idiom
open an account — opens an account — opened an account
   a bank account
   a checking account
   a savings account
   a charge account

UNIT 15

Paragraph Completion

A. This paragraph completion exercise is a little different from the others that you have done. This time the teacher will read an expository paragraph instead of a story. The paragraph is about wigs.

You may ask questions about anything you do not understand. You may also ask the teacher to write on the board any words that are new to you.

When you are familiar with the selection, the teacher will give you a written form that contains blanks to be filled in. This time, however, you will need to fill in more words. Two blanks require several words. Listen carefully to the reading.

Identifying Topics

B. In Unit 9 you wrote a paragraph about the development of watches. When you read the sentences that were given, however, you found that they were really about two different topics. The topic sentence was about watches, but some of the sentences were about clocks. You had to select the sentences about watches.

EXERCISE

In this exercise the sentences also deal with two different topics. See if you can decide what the two topics are. Follow the directions.

Directions: Read all the sentences. Then go back and read the sentences again, marking them A or B according to the topic they belong to. After you have finished, write the two topics. You need *not* write topic sentences. Just write the two topics in brief form on the blank lines below the sentences.

Sentences
1. The developments in modern postal services came chiefly from Great Britain.
2. Before postage stamps were used, the person who received a letter had to pay the postage.
3. Another excellent way of obtaining stamps is by exchanging stamps with other collectors.

111

UNIT 15

4. As the collection grows, more pages and then more albums are needed.
5. Finally stamps were put on sale to the public in 1840.
6. Once this start has been made, it is not difficult to add to the collection.
7. At first they were printed in sheets and had to be cut apart by scissors.
8. One development was the use of postage stamps.
9. The next requirement is a stamp album.
10. The ancient Egyptians, Persians, Greeks, and Romans all had postal services.
11. Relatives and friends who live overseas or go abroad can be a great help.
12. Many collectors use loose-leaf albums.
13. The idea of a postal service is very old.
14. Friends who are office workers can also help, for many offices receive letters from abroad every day.
15. Such a packet bought from a shop contains only common stamps, but they will be clean and in good condition.
16. In England Sir Rowland Hill got the idea of postage stamps which could be bought at the post office and stuck on the letter by the person who sent the letter.
17. The best way for a beginner to obtain a stock of stamps is to buy a packet of 500 or 1000 mixed stamps from a stamp shop.
18. The idea of making little holes, or perforations, between the stamps so that they could be torn apart easily without using scissors was first used in 1854 in Great Britain.
19. After the first purchase, you may want to buy your stamps from a post office instead of from a stamp shop.
20. It required a long time for Hill to convince the government that his idea was a good one.

The two topics are: a. _____
                    b. _____

Identifying Supporting Details

C. This exercise will give you more practice with supporting details. Again you are to list the essential points that support the topic sentence. Follow the same procedure that you did in Unit 14. However, you will find these paragraphs a little more difficult than those in Unit 14. In those paragraphs each sentence added an essential point, but in these paragraphs there are extra sentences and you will have to look more carefully for the *main* supporting details.

1. A space suit will help a traveler to the moon in various ways. It will protect him from very high and very low temperatures. It will have tanks filled with air to breathe. People from earth cannot live with just the thin air of the moon. The space suit will also have

UNIT 15

heavy shoes to help in walking. These are necessary because the moon does not have as much gravity as the earth does.

_____
_____
_____
_____
_____

2. As transportation has improved, the movement of mail has been speeded up. Trains are commonly used for transporting mail. Where trains do not go, the mail is carried by trucks or cars. The greatest advance in speed came with the use of airplanes. Airmail service is now available around the globe. To speed up mail deliveries even more, the postal service has been using helicopters in recent years. Mail trucks frequently get slowed by heavy traffic, but helicopters can carry mail quickly from the airport to the roof of a post office in the center of the city.

_____
_____
_____
_____
_____

3. Before the scientific age, people had many strange ideas about rain. Some people thought that it was water which came from above the sky. They thought that the sky had windows, and when the windows were open water came down to the earth. Other people thought that certain gods controlled the rain. These people would do special dances and give presents to the gods. They thought that if they made the gods happy, rain would come. One group of people believed that frogs controlled the rain. These people wanted rain, but they did not try to make frogs happy. Instead, they hit the frogs with sticks. They thought that if they made the frogs afraid, the frogs would make it rain.

_____
_____
_____
_____
_____

UNIT 15

STRUCTURE EXERCISE:
Review

D. 1. Here are the irregular verbs that you practiced in Unit 11. Do you remember the past tense of these verbs?

begin	drive	know
bring	eat	lose
buy	find	make
do	forget	see
drink	get	write

2. Here is another way to practice these verbs. Use this sentence:

He _____ it yesterday.

The teacher will give you the present form of a verb and you will repeat the sentence, filling the blank with the correct form of the verb.

More Irregular Verbs

3. Here are some more common irregular verbs. Can you give the past tense?

bite	leave	spend
catch	mean	steal
choose	pay	teach
feel	run	tell
fly	sell	throw
hear	send	understand

4. Now practice using the verbs in section 3 with the sentence in section 2.

STRUCTURE EXERCISE

E. 1. You know that nouns, verbs, and adjectives occur in certain positions in sentences. What is the position for adverbs? Look at these sentences:

a. He walked *slowly*.
b. He walked *slowly* to the corner.
c. He drove *carefully*.
d. He drove the car *carefully*.
e. He ran *fast*.
f. He studied *hard* for the exam.

In these sentences the adverb occurs at the end of the sentence or after the verb. These are common positions for adverbs. In each of these sentences the adverb modifies the verb.

Adverbs may also occur in other positions. There are various kinds of adverbs. In fact, there is a great deal of variety in adverbs and their position in sentences. You will learn more about them as you progress in writing.

The adverbs in the example sentence tell *how* something is done. (Adverbs may also tell *where, when, how much,* or *why.*) Many adverbs end in -*ly,* but some of them do not; notice the adverbs *fast* and *hard*. In your spelling lists you have had some other adverbs that do not end in -*ly*. What are they?

UNIT 15

EXERCISE

2. Fill in suitable adverbs in the following sentences:

a. She ate her supper _____.

b. The students copied the paragraph _____.

c. Many people drive _____.

d. The batter hit the ball _____.

e. He spoke _____ to his brother.

EXERCISE

3. Make sentences that use these adverbs: *rapidly, loudly, cheerfully, angrily, often, well, poorly.*

STRUCTURE EXERCISE AND COPYREADING

F. You have had exercises in which you identified complete and incomplete sentences. In this exercise you are to identify complete sentences and then put in periods and capital letters. The exercise is both a sentence exercise and a copyreading exercise.

Follow the directions carefully.

Directions:
Step 1. Decide where each sentence ends and put a period there.
Step 2. When you are sure you have put the periods in the right places, go back and make a small x on top of the periods, like this: ✗ This will make it easier to find the periods and to correct your paper.
Step 3. After you have placed all the periods and marked them x, capitalize the first word in each sentence that does not already begin with a capital letter.

Jackie Robinson

Jackie Robinson is famous in baseball he was the first black player on a major league team he began to play with the Brooklyn Dodgers in 1947 Jackie had a very difficult time many people thought that only white players should play in the big leagues they soon changed their opinions because Jackie was a wonderful player he belonged in the big leagues he established many baseball records Jackie retired from baseball in 1957 and became a businessman he was 38 years old Jackie Robinson became the first black player to be elected to baseball's Hall of Fame he was elected in 1962

How many sentences are there in this paragraph? _____
How many capital letters did you put in? _____

115

UNIT 15

Spelling Review

G. 1. The following sentences contain *ie* and *ei* words that you have had in spelling lists or as examples. How many can you fill in correctly?

a. Jimmy ate a very large p _ _ ce of cake.

b. The Johnsons are unhappy. They dented a fender on th _ _ r new car.

c. Students sometimes try to dec _ _ ve a teacher.

d. When Ethel is on a trip, she usually sends postcards to her fr _ _ nds.

e. Mr. Miller has a stiff neck today because he painted the c _ _ ling of the living room yesterday.

f. Mrs. Morris took some food to her sick n _ _ ghbor.

g. Bud Jones plays right f _ _ ld for the Yankees.

h. Marilyn is on a diet because she w _ _ ghs too much.

i. It is best not to bel _ _ ve everything you hear.

j. Harvey likes to rec _ _ ve letters from for _ _ gn countries because he collects stamps.

Words to Know

2. Here are some useful words to know. You should know their spelling, meaning, and pronunciation.

Nouns
advantage — advantages
length — len<u>g</u>ths
type
Tuesday — Tuesdays
typewriter — typewriters

NOTICE THE <u>g</u>.

Adjectives
serious
personal

Verbs
wear — wears — wore
deliver — delivers — delivered
reco<u>mm</u>end — reco<u>mm</u>ends — reco<u>mm</u>ended

THIS VERB IS IRREGULAR.

Adverb
i<u>m</u>mediately

Idioms
go shopping — goes shopping — went shopping
go window-shopping — goes window-shopping — went window-shopping

Vocabulary Game

H. Here is another vocabulary game, but this one is different from the game you have played before. On a piece of paper draw a diagram like the one below. (You can make yours larger. Make it large enough for you to write words in the spaces.) The class will choose a word containing five letters to write across the top. The example uses the word *chair,* but you may use another word if you wish.

	C	H	A	I	R
nouns	coat				
adjectives					
verbs					
adverbs					

The object of the game is to fill each square with a word beginning with the letter at the top. The word must be the kind of word indicated at the left. One square is filled as an example.

You will have ten minutes in which to fill the squares. Then exchange papers with one of your neighbors and correct the papers. In making corrections, ask the teacher about any words that you are not sure about. The words must be correctly spelled and be the correct part of speech. Each correct word counts 1 point. If any student has a (correct) word that no one else has, he may score 5 points for that word. The student with the highest total score is the winner.

UNIT 16

Paragraph Completion

A. The teacher will read a paragraph two or three times and then give you a written form that contains blanks to be filled in. You may ask questions about anything you do not understand. You may also ask the teacher to write on the board any words that are new to you.

This time the subject of the paragraph is "Votes for Women." Most of the blanks require only one word, but some of them require several words. Listen carefully to the reading.

DEVELOPING THE TOPIC

B. The expository paragraphs you have studied have a topic sentence followed by supporting sentences. The supporting sentences give additional information about the topic sentence. The topic sentence is usually rather general and the supporting details are more specific.

Giving additional information in this way is called *developing the topic. Developing* means explaining the topic, making it clearer to the reader, or convincing the reader that the topic statement is really true. There is more than one way of developing the topic. The kind you have practiced so far consists of additional details; that is, additional facts about the topic.

Developing with Examples

The kind of information in the supporting sentences depends on what is said in the topic sentence. Sometimes the clearest and quickest way to explain a topic sentence is to use an *example*. Look at these pairs of sentences:

1. Many people collect things as a hobby. For example, they may collect stamps, old coins, matchbook covers, dolls, phonograph records, or autographs of famous people.

2. Automation is reducing the number of workers needed in many industries. For instance, in an electronics plant where 200 men used to assemble 1000 units a day, only two men tending automatic machines now turn out just as many.

You see that in these pairs of sentences the first one makes a general statement and the second one illustrates the point with a specific case or cases; that is, with *examples*. Often a good example can make a topic clearer than a long explanation. A writer may use only one example, or he may use several examples (as in paragraph 1). Even though there may be several examples, the expression *for example* or *for instance* is used only once.

Signals of Examples

Notice that you have signals to tell you that these are examples. The signals are the expressions *for example* and *for instance*. However, such signals are not always present in material that you read. You need to recognize examples even when there is no signal. Look at paragraph 1 again, without the signals:

1a. Many people collect things as a hobby. They may collect stamps, old coins, matchbook covers, dolls, phonograph records, or autographs of famous people.

The second sentence consists of examples even though it does not definitely say *for example*.

It is very important for you to recognize examples in your reading. In your writing, you may use your judgment as to whether you wish to use the signals. If you want to make it very clear to the reader that you are using an example, use one of the signals. *For example* and *for instance* are the most common signals for examples, but you will notice others in your reading.

EXERCISE

C. In these paragraphs see if you can identify the examples even though the two common signals are not used. What are the examples?

1. Fashions seem to repeat themselves. In the 1960s men went back to the old style of wearing long hair and long sideburns. During the same period women revived the fashion of wearing wigs.

2. Science has made the world very different today from what it was one hundred years ago. Today we can travel around the world in only a few hours. We can talk to people who are in another city or another country. When it is dark, we can easily turn on an electric light.

3. Machines are so much a part of our everyday lives that it is hard to imagine life without them. Suppose you had to wash your clothes by hand instead of using an electric washing machine. Imagine what an office would be like if there were no typewriters. Imagine getting along without automobiles, buses, trucks, and airplanes.

UNIT 16

EXERCISE

D. Give examples that would illustrate these topic sentences. You need not give sentences. Just write the example you can think of on the blank lines.

1. Many of the small cars used in the United States come from foreign countries.
   _____
   _____
   _____

2. Many of the greatest stars in sports today are black.
   _____
   _____
   _____

3. Some of the most popular public entertainers today are women.
   _____
   _____
   _____

4. Some of the leading baseball players today are from Latin America.
   _____
   _____
   _____

Punctuation

E. When you use *for example* and *for instance,* you must remember to use commas with them. The rule is similar to Punctuation Rule 2 for the use of *however.*

Punctuation Rule (2a): The Comma

Use a comma after the expression *for example* (and *for instance*) when it begins a sentence.
Use two commas, one before and one after, when *for example* occurs inside a sentence.
Use a comma before *for example* when it occurs at the end of a sentence.

UNIT 16

Examples: *Many people collect things as a hobby.*
For example, some people collect stamps.
Some people, for example, collect stamps.
Some people collect stamps, for example.

"Scrambled" Paragraphs

F. You are to arrange the sentences in good order to make coherent paragraphs. First find the sentence that seems best for the topic sentence. Then look for signals (sentence links) that show you how the other sentences fit together. Write the correct order in which the sentences should come in the paragraphs.

1.
1. The White House is a very large building.
2. His official home is called the White House.
3. Some of the rooms are open to the public.
4. The President of the United States lives and works in a special residence.
5. It contains reception rooms, offices, and rooms in which the President's family lives.

____ , ____ , ____ , ____ , ____

2.
1. These machines are clever salesmen.
2. Machines that provide service include washing machines, copying machines, and juke boxes.
3. They sell both merchandise and service.
4. Their merchandise includes cigarettes, candy, gum, soft drinks, sandwiches, and many other items.
5. Vending machines are common in today's world.

____ , ____ , ____ , ____ , ____

G. Copy the sentences in section F in the order in which you numbered them, putting them in paragraph form. Copyread your paragraphs before you hand in your paper.

Assignment

WRITING TOPIC SENTENCES

H. In Unit 13 you read several paragraphs and had to decide which of them had topic sentences and which did not. Now you are to write

121

UNIT 16

topic sentences for the paragraphs which do not have them.

Turn back to Unit 13, exercise B, page 94. Read the first paragraph that does *not* have a topic sentence. What is the topic of this paragraph? What can you say about the topic? Fill in the blanks below. Then follow the same steps for the two other paragraphs that do not have topic sentences.

Paragraph _____. Topic: _____

Topic sentence: _____
_____

Paragraph _____. Topic: _____

Topic sentence: _____
_____

Paragraph _____. Topic: _____

Topic sentence: _____
_____

Alphabetical Order

I. You have alphabetized words in which the first two letters were the same. In the following words the first three letters are the same. In some the fourth and fifth letters are the same. How would you alphabetize them?

confuse	conceal	concrete	concert
connect	consent	condition	contain
consonant	contractor	conclusion	conduct
continue	control	contribution	conflict

1. _____   9. _____
2. _____   10. _____
3. _____   11. _____
4. _____   12. _____
5. _____   13. _____
6. _____   14. _____
7. _____   15. _____
8. _____   16. _____

UNIT 16

Words Often Confused

J. The words *to, too,* and *two* are frequently confusing. These sentences will show whether you can use them correctly.

1. It is time to return the book _____ the library.

2. His mother sent the boy _____ to the store for a loaf of bread.

3. That exam was _____ long to finish in an hour.

4. Five students received grades above 90; three were girls and _____ were boys.

5. That tire is _____ thin to drive on. In fact, it is dangerous.

6. The jumper tried the high jump _____ times and failed, but on the third attempt he made it.

7. I couldn't drink the coffee right away because it was _____ hot.

8. The batter was on the spot. _____ men were out and the bases were loaded.

9. She wanted to buy the dress, but she thought it was _____ expensive.

10. Nancy is going to a movie after work, and Janet is going, _____.

Number correct _____

Review   If you made any mistakes, you need to review these words.

to   *To* is a preposition. It is used here with nouns.
    Tony's mother sent a note *to* the teacher.
    The boy went *to* the store for some bread.

too   *Too* is an adverb. It means "more than enough."
    He got sick because he ate *too* much pizza.
    It was *too* cold to play outside, so he watched TV.

    Too has another meaning: *also.*
    Tony was late, and Jimmy was, *too.*
    Betty likes science, and Marilyn does, *too.*

two   *Two* is a number.
    The boys broke *two* windows while they were playing baseball.

UNIT 16

Spelling Review

K. 1. All the words below end in *y*, but notice that some of the words are nouns and some are verbs. Change all the words to their *s* form. Put the nouns in the first column and the verbs in the second column.

	Nouns	Verbs
a. alley	_____	_____
b. enjoy	_____	_____
c. library	_____	_____
d. country	_____	_____
e. pay	_____	_____
f. company	_____	_____
g. difficulty	_____	_____
h. obey	_____	_____
i. salary	_____	_____
j. industry	_____	_____
k. apply	_____	_____

New Rule

2. Here are some words from spelling lists that you have studied. All the words are verbs.

describe	lose	come
notice	decide	ride
believe	organize	recognize
produce	write	receive

Notice that all these verbs end in *e*. However, the *e* is not pronounced (as it is in words like *me, he, see*). You know the spelling of all these verbs, including the *s* form and the past form. The words have another form which you have not yet practiced—the *ing* form.

Examples: When I came to see her, she was <u>writing</u> a letter.
Henry is <u>riding</u> his scooter this afternoon.
Are you <u>coming</u> to the party tonight?

What do you notice about the spelling of the underlined words? You see that when *ing* is added, the *e* is dropped.
Here is the rule:

UNIT 16

Spelling Rule (4)

When a verb ends with a silent *e*, drop the *e* before adding *ing*.

This is an important and useful rule because there are a great many verbs that end with a silent *e*, and the rule applies *most* of the time. (As you know, the rules for spelling usually have some exceptions.)

EXERCISE

3. Fill the blanks with the *ing* form of the word in parentheses.

a. (organize) The congressman is busy _____ his political campaign.

b. (write) He is _____ letters to many voters in his district.

c. (recognize) The congressman is good at _____ people even if he has met them only once or twice.

d. (come) Are you _____ with me to hear the congressman's speech?

e. (lose) The little boy is constantly _____ his shoes.

f. (produce) The company is _____ a new line of merchandise.

g. (describe) The announcer last night was _____ the basketball game very well.

h. (ride) When I saw Henry, he was _____ his scooter.

i. (receive) Barbara is _____ many cards this week because her birthday is next Sunday.

j. (believe) A well-known expression is "Seeing is _____." What does it mean?

Words to Know

4. Here are some useful words to know. You should know their spelling, meaning, and pronunciation.

UNIT 16

	Nouns
	customer — customers
	machine — machines
	service — services
NOTICE THE SILENT d.	We<u>d</u>nesday — We<u>d</u>nesdays
	something — *no plural*

	Adjectives
	several
NOTICE THE SILENT LETTERS.	strai<u>gh</u>t

	Verbs
THIS VERB IS IRREGULAR.	think — thinks — thinking — <u>thought</u>
	imagine — imagines — imagining — imagined

	Adverb
NOTICE THE DOUBLE LETTERS.	real<u>l</u>y

UNIT 17

Paragraph Completion

A. Again the teacher will read a paragraph until you are familiar with it and then will give you a written form with blanks to be filled in. You may ask questions during the reading about words that are new to you, or about anything else that you do not understand.

This time the paragraph is about banks. Most of the blanks require only one word, but one blank requires several words. You will also have to complete the last sentence in the paragraph. Listen carefully to the way the paragraph ends.

More About Examples

B. In the last unit you began to learn about the use of examples in developing topic sentences. If you can recognize examples in your reading, it will help you to use examples in your writing. Look at these paragraphs.

1. The book is on the desk. It is a large book. It is new. It is a chemistry book.

2. Thomas A. Edison was an American inventor. He was born in Ohio in 1847. Throughout his life he worked in various technical and scientific fields. He became very successful and famous. He is especially famous for inventing the electric light.

In these paragraphs you can see that the supporting sentences are not examples. They give additional pieces of information about the topic.

Now compare paragraph 2 with this paragraph.

3. The ideas of Thomas A. Edison, who was one of the world's great inventors, affect almost every part of our lives. When we pick up a telephone, we are using some of his ideas. When we turn on an electric light, we are benefiting by his ideas. When we put a record on a phonograph or watch a movie, we are enjoying the results of his ideas. His inventions had an important effect on the whole field of electricity.

UNIT 17

You can see that in paragraph 3 some of the sentences give examples. Which are the sentences that give examples?

It is quite easy for you to pick out the examples in this paragraph. Sometimes it is very clear which supporting details are examples and which are not. At other times it is not clear. Sometimes the only difference between an additional detail and an example is that one *is called* an example. Look at this paragraph, which you read early in these units:

4. John is a very good student. He does his homework every night. His notebook is neat. He is always able to answer correctly when the teacher calls on him. He usually gets an A on examinations.

When we studied this paragraph earlier, we said that the supporting sentences gave additional details. This is true. In this case, however, the additional details are the kind that could also be considered examples. Notice that if you add *for example* or *for instance*, the supporting details will serve as examples:

4a. John is a very good student. For example, he does his homework every night. His notebook is neat. He is always able to answer correctly when the teacher calls on him. He usually gets an A on examinations.

It is not particularly important whether a supporting point is called an additional fact or an example. The important thing is to provide a specific detail that really supports the topic sentence; that is, makes it more understandable or more convincing to the reader.

Assignment

C. Turn back to Unit 16, exercise D. In that exercise you were given topic sentences and you listed examples of each one. Now you are to choose one of the topic sentences and write a paragraph using the examples listed. (You should have at least three examples.) Write at least one sentence about each example. If you have enough information to write more than one sentence about each example, that is even better.

First make a rough draft. Then make a neat copy to hand in. Copyread your paragraph before you hand it in. Did you indent the first line?

UNIT 17

Copyreading

D. In this copyreading exercise you must look for several kinds of errors. There are errors in punctuation, capitalization, and grammar (the form of nouns and verbs). However, there is only one error in each sentence. How many errors can you find? Make your corrections neatly.

Vending Machines

A vending machine is a device that gives a products or service when a coin is put in a slot. There are many kind of vending machines. Some of them sell merchandise such as candy, gum peanuts, and cigarettes. big companies often have machines that sell various kinds of food. For example they sell soup, sandwiches, hot coffee, cold drinks, and ice cream. Many large airports has machines that sell travel insurance policies. Machines that provide service include washing machines drycleaning machines, and copying machines. Copying machines, which make copies of printed or typewritten material, were very popular now. Coin machines is becoming more efficient all the time. Many of them even makes change.

How many commas did you add? _____

How many capital letters did you add? _____

How many nouns did you change? _____

How many verbs did you change? _____

Spelling

E. 1. Do you remember the little "poem" in Unit 14 about spelling *ie* and *ei* words? If you do not remember it, turn back to Unit 14, section M. Also review the words discussed in that section.

Below are some sentences containing words that have not been in spelling lists but that are probably familiar to you. The teacher will read each sentence two or three times. Listen to the sound of the words containing blanks. Can you fill in the blanks with *ei* or *ie* correctly?

a. A th _ _ f on the subway stole my money.

b. Angela is my sister's daugher. That makes her my n _ _ ce.

UNIT 17

c. The nurse took the blood from a v _ _ n in my arm.

d. The man in the car over there is the ch _ _ f of police.

e. Every policeman wears a sh _ _ ld on his uniform.

f. I would guess that her w _ _ ght is about 120 pounds.

g. A business letter should usually be br _ _ f.

h. The women of the family wore black v _ _ ls at the funeral.

i. The pr _ _ st conducts mass at the church at six o'clock every morning.

j. A great deal of fr _ _ ght is shipped by truck.

Review

2. Write the *ing* form of these verbs:

a. explain _____   f. deliver _____
b. accept _____   g. imagine _____
c. write _____   h. wear _____
d. appear _____   i. decide _____
e. advertise _____   j. come _____

Words to Know

3. Here are some useful words for you to know. You should know their meaning, pronunciation, and spelling.

Nouns
minute — minutes

NOTICE THE SILENT p.
rece<u>i</u>pt — rece<u>i</u>pts
development — developments
condition — conditions

Adjectives
natural
<u>e</u>ssential

Verbs
THIS VERB IS IRREGULAR.
do — does — doing — <u>did</u>
require — requires — requiring — required
contribute — contributes — contributing — contributed

Adverb
formerly

UNIT 17

Game

F. This is the same vocabulary game that you played in Unit 15. Draw a rectangle on a piece of paper and divide it into boxes, five across and four down. The class will choose a five-letter word to write across the top, one letter above each square. Down the left side write the words *nouns, adjectives, verbs,* and *adverbs.* The teacher will tell you how much time you have in which to fill the boxes with suitable words. Follow the same procedure that you did before for correcting and scoring the papers.

Assignment

G. You are to write a paragraph using the material you had previously on the development of postal services. Turn back to Unit 15, exercise B, page 111. Then follow the directions below.

Directions:
1. Use sentence 1 as your topic sentence: *The developments in modern postal services came chiefly from Great Britain.*
2. Mark all the sentences that are relevant to the topic.
3. Rearrange the sentences to put them in good order in the paragraph. Use sentence links as signals to guide you in doing this.
4. When you have rearranged the sentences, count them. You should have eight sentences. If you have more than this, you have some that are irrelevant and should be taken out.
5. Copy your paragraph neatly to hand in.
6. Copyread your paragraph carefully.

UNIT 18

A DICTO-COMP

A. Today you will have a new kind of exercise called a *dicto-comp*. This kind of exercise is called a dicto-comp because it is partly like dictation and partly like writing a composition. First you will listen to a short, easy story. Then you will write the story.

You have done several paragraph completion exercises in which you filled in blanks in the written form of the story or paragraph. Now, in the dicto-comp, you will write the whole story. It will be necessary to listen carefully to the reading.

The teacher will read the story as many times as you wish. The teacher will answer questions about the story and spell any words you do not know. All this will make the selection very familiar to you. Then you will write the story. Try to write it in the same words and sentences that the teacher used. However, if you do not remember the teacher's words exactly, use your own words.

Copyreading

When you finish writing the story, copyread it before handing it in to the teacher.

Sentence Links: Review

B. 1. You are now familiar with several kinds of links between sentences. Here are examples of those you have studied so far.

a. *If you go to the moon, you will have to wear a space suit. A space suit is necessary to protect you from the intense heat and the intense cold.*

b. *Your space suit will help you in another way. It will have tanks of air.*

c. *Maxine was late for work. Her car broke down.*

d. *Your space suit will have heavy shoes. These shoes will help you to talk on the moon.*

e. *Several diseases are commonly called children's diseases. These include measles, chicken pox, and whooping cough.*

UNIT 18

Underline the sentence links in these examples. Then identify the *kind* of sentence link that each example illustrates.

2. Still another kind of sentence link is illustrated in the next examples. In each example, there are two words that have the same meaning. Underline these words.

a. *Once there was a man who knew a rich merchant. One day he asked the merchant, "How did you become so wealthy?"*

b. *One reason for the increased number of accidents on the roads is the increased number of automobiles. Twice as many cars are on the roads as three years ago.*

c. *We continue to pay taxes to build more roads. In spite of new highways, traffic is as bad as ever.*

Synonyms

You will notice that instead of repeating a key word, the second sentence in each example uses a *synonym*. A synonym is a word that means the same, or almost the same, as another word. A synonym is another kind of substitute word; that is, it is used to avoid repeating a word or expression in a previous sentence. Synonyms give variety to writing.

It is not always possible to use a synonym, for all words do not have synonyms. When there is a good synonym, however, it can be used for variety.

EXERCISE

3. The examples in this exercise use synonyms. Underline the words in each example that have similar meanings.

a. Two men were walking along a river bank when they heard a loud cry. They listened and discovered that someone was struggling in the water ahead of them. They ran in the direction of the shout. One of the men plunged into the river and saved a boy from drowning.

b. There would be fewer accidents if drivers were more cautious. Many accidents occur when one car tries to pass another. A careful driver never passes a car unless he sees that the road ahead is clear.

c. Galileo, an early scientist, had ideas that were different from those of most men in his day. In fact, he was far ahead of his time. Consequently it was dangerous for him to discuss his opinions.

d. When transportation depended mainly on the horse, it was not very fast. It became much faster when the automobile was invented. With the coming of the airplane, transportation became even more speedy.

UNIT 18

EXERCISE

4. Can you put a suitable synonym in the blanks?

a. When I want vegetables, I always go to a shop on Benton Street. That _____ is sure to have vegetables that are really fresh.

b. My neighbor has a very big dog, a German shepherd. It must take a lot of food to feed such a _____ dog.

c. Last night a group of loud boys had an argument on the street outside my window. They were so _____ that they woke me up.

d. I wanted a new dress for the party, but I wanted an inexpensive one. I went to a shop I know about that carries a lot of attractive but _____ dresses.

e. Jose is so handsome that he never has any trouble getting dates. A fellow as _____ as Jose is always popular with girls.

f. My mother is a very fine cook. My brother Walter says he wants to find a wife who will also be an _____ cook. Perhaps that is why he is thirty years old and still a bachelor.

Assignment:
Relevance and Coherence

C. Again you are to choose supporting details for topic sentences. This time, however, you will have *two* topic sentences instead of one. From the additional sentences given, you are to make two paragraphs. Select sentences that go with each topic sentence.

First look at the two topic sentences. What kind of information should probably follow Sentence A? What kind of information should probably follow Sentence B? Now follow the directions.

Topic sentences:
   A. The beverage called coffee is produced from the seeds of an evergreen bush or small tree.
   B. The use of coffee has spread throughout the world.

Additional sentences:
1. Coffee originated in Ethiopia hundreds of years ago.
2. From Ethiopia it was taken to Arabia.
3. Coffee trees need a warm climate.
4. Those grown at a high altitude produce the best quality of coffee.
5. Until the 17th century it was grown mostly in Yemen, in southern Arabia.
6. It was introduced into Turkey in the 1500s and became popular in Europe in the 1600s.
7. The seeds of coffee are called beans.
8. The Dutch began growing coffee in Java in the 1600s and they distributed plants to several other countries.

134

9. They are dried, roasted and ground to produce the familiar drink.
10. The English took coffee to the island of Jamaica.
11. The coffee we drink is usually a combination of beans from several areas, blended to produce the desired flavor.
12. Coffee contains a drug called caffeine which stimulates the nervous system.
13. From there coffee was taken to Central and South America.
14. Some people cannot drink it in the evening for it makes them sleepless.
15. It was first grown in Brazil in the early 1700s.
16. Now Brazil is the world's largest producer of coffee.
17. Other people are not affected by it.

Directions:
(1) Read all the additional sentences.
(2) Go back and read the sentences again, marking them A or B according to the topic sentence they fit best.
(3) Then make a paragraph using topic sentence A and its supporting sentences. Check the sentence links to make sure that the supporting sentences are in good order.
(4) Make another paragraph using topic sentence B and its supporting sentences. Again, use the sentence links to check the order of the supporting sentences.
(5) Count the number of sentences you have in each paragraph. Paragraph A should have nine sentences and paragraph B should have ten.
(6) Make a neat copy of your two paragraphs and copyread them before you hand them in.

D. 1. You are to make sentences from the vocabulary given below. This exercise gives you practice in using the *ing* form of verbs.

STRUCTURE EXERCISE

Examples: *Paul   throw   the ball   Dick   catch   it*
<u>Paul is throwing the ball, and Dick is catching it.</u>

This evening   Bill   go   to the library   Jim   walk the dog
<u>This evening Bill is going to the library, and Jim is walking the dog.</u>

Look at the examples carefully. Notice the changes that have been made in the underlined sentences. Now do the exercise orally, using the words to make similar sentences.

Using the ing *form*

a. This morning   Harry   work   on his car   George   fix   his spare tire
b. Today is a hot day. Some people go   to the beach   others   go   to a movie
c. This afternoon   Mercedes   wash   her hair   her brother Edward   wash   his car
d. Miriam and Sally are at home this evening. Miriam   sewing   Sally   knit   a sweater
e. This afternoon   Mrs. Jackson   buy   groceries   Danny   carry   them   for her

UNIT 18

f. This afternoon Peter and the other boys are at the park. Peter   play   tennis   the others   ride   their bicycles
g. This evening   Dave   watch   baseball   on TV   his brother   do   his homework
h. This morning   a policewoman   tag   cars   on that side   of the street   another   tag   cars   on this side

2. Now can you make up some sentences of your own, using the same structure?

Spelling

E. 1. You know that when a verb ends in silent *e* (like *come*), you drop the *e* before you add *ing* (*coming*). But what do you do when you add *ing* to verbs that do not end in silent *e*? For example:

    run   stop   put   swim
    hop   drop   hit   plan

This is a special group of short verbs that often cause trouble in spelling. Notice three things about them:

(1) They have only one syllable.
(2) They end in one consonant.
(3) They have one vowel before the final consonant.

New Rule

In verbs that have these three features, you *double the consonant* before you add *ing*.

Many people make mistakes with these words because they forget to double the consonant. Since all of them are common words, you need to know how to spell them correctly. To help you remember them, write the *ing* form of them now.

a. drop _____   e. put _____
b. hit _____   f. run _____
c. hop _____   g. stop _____
d. plan _____   h. swim _____

Spelling Rule (5):

When a one-syllable verb ends in one vowel and one consonant, double the consonant before adding *ing*.

UNIT 18

Review

2. These sentences use words that you have had in spelling lists. How many words can you fill in correctly?

Myrna

Myrna is a young w _ _ _ _ who lives in the a _ _ _ _ _ _ _ _ _ next to me; that is, she is my n _ _ _ _ _ _ _. She is a very p _ _ _ _ _ girl. In fact, she is so p _ _ _ _ _ that she should be on the cover of a m _ _ _ _ _ _ _. She has a good job in an office because she is an e _ _ _ _ _ _ _ _ typist. However, Myrna is ambitious and she wants a better job. She does not earn e _ _ _ _ _ money in this job, she says. She has d _ _ _ _ _ _ to learn shorthand. Consequently she is studying shorthand at n _ _ _ _. She goes to class two evenings a week, on T _ _ _ _ _ _ and W _ _ _ _ _ _ _ _. She is learning fast. She can a _ _ _ _ _ _ _ take dictation at 30 words per m _ _ _ _ _.

Words to Know

3. Here are some useful words for you to know. You should know their meaning, pronunciation, and spelling.

Nouns
Monday — Mondays
position — positions
month — months
reference — references

Adjectives
recent
prompt   NOTICE THE SILENT p.

Verbs
type — types — typing — typed
find — finds — finding — <u>found</u>   THIS VERB IS IRREGULAR.

Adverbs
consequently
yesterday

UNIT 18

F. 1. Read this paragraph:

Assignment

    Many of the things we use are made of rubber. The tires on cars are made of rubber. The boots that we wear in rainy weather are usually made of rubber. Some people wear rubber soles on their shoes. The erasers on the end of pencils are also made of rubber.

    Notice that the supporting sentences are examples. Your assignment is to write a paragraph similar to this one. Begin your paragraph with this topic sentence:

Many of the things we use are made of plastic.

You should have at least four supporting sentences, each giving an example of things we use that are made of plastic.
    Copyread your composition before you hand it in.
  2. Study the following paragraph carefully and be prepared to take dictation of it.

Dictation

Superstitions

    People in ancient times had strange ideas and superstitions, and many people still believe in them today. There are many kinds of superstitions. One kind is about things that bring bad luck. For example, if you spill salt or break a mirror, you will have bad luck. It is bad luck to walk under a ladder or open an umbrella in the house. It is also bad luck to kill a spider. Many people believe that the number 13 is unlucky. Friday the 13th is considered an especially unlucky day. It is surprising how many ideas like these have lasted until these modern times.

UNIT 19

Dictation

A. Do the dictation that was assigned in the preceding unit.

DEVELOPING THE TOPIC

B. Read the two paragraphs below. Can you see any difference in the way the topic sentences are developed?

1. Many Americans collect things as a hobby. Some collect works of art, such as paintings or carvings. Others collect stamps or old coins, or even matchbook covers. Some collect books and others collect dolls. Another popular hobby at the present time is collecting phonograph records.

2. Why are men interested in traveling to the moon? One reason is that there is adventure in space travel. Another is that knowledge of the moon can provide valuable scientific information. Still another reason is that they simply want to get there before someone else does.

Since you have had a similar paragraph before, you know that the supporting sentences in paragraph 1 give examples. In paragraph 2, there is a signal that indicates what kind of information is given in the supporting sentences. What is the signal? In fact, there is more than one signal. What other signals do you notice?

Reasons

In paragraph 2, the supporting sentences give *reasons*. The first signal is in the second sentence, which begins: *One reason is* . . . The next signal is in the third sentence, which begins: *Another is* . . . Here the word *reason* is not actually present, but it is understood; the meaning is: Another (reason) is . . . The next signal is in the last sentence, which begins: *Still another reason is* . . .

There is still another signal, a very important one. This time the topic sentence is a question, and it begins with "Why." A question that begins with "Why" requires an answer that gives reasons.

Suppose a friend asks you, "Why do you shop at the Fair Deal Supermarket?" You may answer like this: "I shop there because prices are a little lower than those at the Buy Rite Market across the street." Your answer gives a reason.

If you think for a moment about any of the questions below, you will see that all of them require reasons in the answer:

139

Why do we have traffic lights?
Why is it hard to get a taxi on a rainy day?
Why must all car owners have insurance?
Why are there so many car accidents on the Fourth of July?

A question that begins with "Why" is therefore a signal for reasons. Sometimes, however, there is no clear signal like this. More often the topic sentence is *not* a question beginning with "Why." Instead it may be a statement that makes the reader ask himself "Why?" Look at this example:

3. Good roads are important for a country. They are good for business because they make possible the fast transportation of food and merchandise. They make it possible for people to reach their place of work easily. They also encourage tourism.

As soon as the reader reads the topic sentence, he probably wonders, "*Why* are good roads important for a country?" The writer must immediately answer the reader's mental question by giving reasons.

Another important point is that the supporting statements do not always include the word *reason*. Notice that paragraph 2 includes this signal but paragraph 3 does not. (The situation is similar to the use of examples; sometimes a paragraph using an example includes the signal *for example* or *for instance,* but sometimes it does not.)

EXERCISE

C. Here are several topic sentences. Which of them would you probably develop by using reasons? Mark these with an X.

_____ 1. One of the most important books a person can own is a dictionary.
_____ 2. First impressions of a person are sometimes wrong.
_____ 3. I am glad I am living now instead of a hundred years ago.
_____ 4. Maria helps her mother a great deal with the housework.
_____ 5. A small car is more practical than a large one.
_____ 6. The things that machines can do become more and more remarkable.
_____ 7. Women should not be allowed to become baseball umpires.
_____ 8. Sometimes animals seem to have intelligence similar to that of human beings.
_____ 9. Some of the things we regard as necessities today were not even thought of a few years ago.
_____ 10. Congress should do more to increase the use of public transportation.

UNIT 19

EXERCISE

D. The following paragraphs were developed by reasons. List the reasons given in each sentence. You need not write complete sentences.

1. Most Americans would benefit by doing more walking. Doctors say that walking is one of the best forms of exercise. In good weather, a walk is a pleasant form of recreation. When you are feeling lonely or depressed, a long walk can do a lot to cheer you up.

   _____

   _____

   _____

2. Shopping on Saturday is usually difficult. Many people are doing their shopping on the same day, and the stores are crowded. Customers often have to wait, for the clerks are very busy. Frequently there are not enough clerks. For these reasons some people prefer to shop on other days of the week.

   _____

   _____

   _____

3. People vote for political candidates for various reasons. Some people vote for a candidate because he favors policies that will benefit them personally. Some people vote for a candidate because they like his looks and personality, or because they dislike his opponent's looks and personality. Some people vote for a man simply because he is the candidate of their party.

   _____

   _____

   _____

   _____

STRUCTURE EXERCISE
AND COPYREADING

E. This exercise is similar to one you had before. There are no periods in the following paragraph. You must decide where each sentence ends and the next one begins. Follow the directions carefully.

Directions:
1. Decide where each sentence ends and put a period there.
2. When you have read all the sentences and are sure you have put the periods in the right places, make a small *x* on top of the periods. This is to make it easier to find the periods when your paper is corrected.
3. After you have put in all the periods, capitalize the first word in each sentence that does not already begin with a capital letter.

UNIT 19

The Importance of Salt

We use salt every day and never think about it we would miss it very much, however, if we did not have it our food would taste very flat and uninteresting salt has been important to mankind ever since history began in early times it was an important article of trade at one time salt was so scarce and so valuable that it was used as money Roman soldiers received part of their pay in salt this part of their pay was called *salarium* from this we get our word *salary* in these modern times salt is used in many ways for example, it is used to make glass, soap, washing compounds, and many other products

How many sentences are there in this paragraph? _____

How many capital letters did you put in? _____

Dividing Words Between Syllables

F. 1. You have learned three rules about dividing words at the end of a line. Apply these rules to the words in the following list. If a word should not be divided, write *NO* on the line. If a word has not been covered by the rules you have learned so far, do not write anything on the line.

a. across _____   g. often _____

b. wear _____   h. reference _____

c. able _____   i. find _____

d. possible _____   j. recommend _____

e. application _____   k. many _____

f. over _____   l. only _____

2. Now here is another rule to follow.

Rule for Dividing Words (4): When a word has two consonants together, divide the word between the consonants (except in special cases, explained below).

Examples: *sup-ply*   *dif-ficulty*
           con-nection   *recom-mend*

UNIT 19

Caution: You must be careful in using this rule. It does not apply to every word with double consonants. If a word *ends* with two consonants and you add an ending (such as *ing*), you divide between the original word and the ending.

Examples: *spell-ing, kill-ing, miss-ing*

Remember: If you do not know for sure how to divide a word, either look in a dictionary or write the entire word on the next line.

Alphabetical Order

G. 1. When you have looked up names in the telephone directory, you have noticed that the names are alphabetized according to the last name. If several persons have the same last name, the alphabetical order is according to the first name. If two persons have the same last and first names, the order is according to the middle initial (if there is one). For example:

>Brown, Robert
>Jones, Arthur T.
>Smith, Walter N.
>Smith, Walter S.
>Smith, William

2. Here are some personal names. Arrange them in alphabetical order as a directory would arrange them.

Harry J. Roberts	Ethel M. Duncan
Alice Gibson	Ramon Rodriguez
Henry L. Shelby	Timothy Fair
Andrew Fisher	Delbert H. Owens
Larry Clark	Arthur G. Anderson

(1) _____ (6) _____

(2) _____ (7) _____

(3) _____ (8) _____

(4) _____ (9) _____

(5) _____ (10) _____

UNIT 19

Spelling

H. 1. Write the *ing* form of these verbs.

a. produce _____   f. describe _____

b. plan _____   g. connect _____

c. lose _____   h. run _____

d. recommend _____   i. come _____

e. stop _____   j. put _____

Words to Know

2. Here are some useful words for you to know. You should know their meaning, spelling, and pronunciation.

Nouns
secretary — secretaries
insurance — *no plural*
policy — policies
January — *plural seldom used*

Adjective
origin<u>al</u>

Verbs
NOTICE THE SILENT g.   sign — signs — signing — signed
watch — watches — watching — watched
enclose — encloses — enclosing — enclosed
THIS VERB IS IRREGULAR.   take — takes — taking — <u>took</u>

Adverb
tomo<u>rr</u>ow

I. This assignment will give you more practice in writing business letters.

Assignment: Letter Writing

A TV commercial has been advertising a sale of records. Write a letter ordering a record or records, following the correct form for business letters. Say that you are enclosing a money order or check and state the amount. The address given in the TV commercial is: RECORDS, Box 8429, New York, NY 10017. Three kinds of records are for sale. You may order one item, two items, or all three items: "Rock Classics" $3.95; "Spanish Favorites" $2.50; "Alltime Popular Favorites" $1.95.

UNIT 20

A Dicto-comp

A. This unit begins with another dicto-comp. The procedure will be the same as for the previous ones. The teacher will read a short selection several times and you will listen to it. Then you will try to write it in the same words that the teacher used. If you cannot remember the words exactly, use your own words.

This time the selection will not be a story. Instead, it will be a short, easy paragraph about small cars. Notice how the paragraph is developed.

The title of the selection is "Small Cars." Write this title on your paper and then listen to the reading.

IDENTIFYING REASONS

B. Some of the paragraphs that follow are developed by reasons and some are not. See if you can identify those that are developed by reasons. Mark them with R.

_____ 1. Some people like to paint furniture or the rooms in their house, but I do not enjoy it. It takes a long time to get the paint mixed. It is hard to apply the paint evenly; it always seems to streak. The paint gets on my clothes, my arms, and sometimes my face. I also drop it from the brush and have to wipe it from places where it is not supposed to be.

_____ 2. Ice cream is so common in our lives that we never think about how we happened to have it. Who first made ice cream? It is thought that ice cream, like many other things, originated in China. It is believed that Marco Polo, a famous traveler, brought the idea from China to Italy several centuries ago. From Italy it spread to France and England, and later to the United States.

_____ 3. The idea behind credit cards is that someone trusts us and believes that we will pay for something at a later date. The use of credit in business is very old. People have given other people credit for thousands of years in many different parts of the world. The modern credit card, however, has been in use only since about 1950. People use credit cards for food, lodging, goods and services of all kinds.

UNIT 20

_____ 4. It is not surprising that Roy's grades are low. Although he is bright, he does not apply himself; that is, he does not work hard enough. He does not have much perseverance, either; if a subject becomes a little difficult, he will not finish it. And, last but not least, he always does his school work at the last minute, so of course he never does a thorough job.

_____ 5. Most of the small, common conveniences we have came into existence because someone in the past had a bright idea. Before someone had the idea of postage stamps, sending a letter was very inconvenient. The person who thought of the paper clip has helped everyone who has worked in an office since then. And the person who got the idea of the of the safety pin made another small but important contribution.

Copyreading

C. In this copyreading exercise you must look for several kinds of errors. There are errors in punctuation, capitalization, and grammar (the form of nouns, verbs, and pronouns). Also, two words are spelled incorrectly. How many errors can you find? Make your corrections neatly.

NOTE: In this exercise, *some sentences have more than one error.*

Useful Small Articles

Machines are very important in modern life. However many small article are also convenient and necessary. For example think about the postage stamp. It is very convenient to use a stamps instead of paying for each letter at the post office. another item is the straight pin. It is very small, but they are very useful. The safety pins is another handy small article. the inventor of the safety pin was a very clever persons. Another clever person invent the paper clip Paper clips are very simple and very small, but they are necesary in offices

How many punctuation marks did you put in? _____
How many capital letters did you put in? _____
How many verbs did you change? _____
How many nouns did you change? _____

UNIT 20

How many pronouns did you change? _____

Is this paragraph developed by reasons? _____

What is the correct spelling of the two words that were spelled incorrectly?

_____

_____

EXERCISE

D. Now you are to write a paragraph of your own using reasons. You will do this in class. The title will be:

      Why I Am Attending This Class

Follow the directions.

Directions:
Step 1. Think about your reasons. List each one of them briefly, just as you listed the reasons in Unit 19, exercise D.
Step 2. Then think about your topic sentence. Do you have several reasons, two reasons, or only one reason? It will make a difference in how you express the topic sentence. The teacher will help classmembers in deciding what to say in their topic sentences.
Step 3. When you have written your topic sentence, write your supporting sentences, using the reasons you listed above. This time, of course, you are able to write complete sentences.
Step 4. Go over your sentences and change and improve them all you can, for this is a rough draft. You may ask questions of the teacher.

Assignment

E. As homework, make a neat copy of your paragraph. Copyread your composition carefully. Did you indent the first line? Does every sentence begin with a capital letter and end with a period? In each sentence, does the verb agree with the subject? Is every word spelled correctly? Did you divide any words, at the end of a line, that should not be divided?

Following Directions

F. This exercise will show how well you can follow directions. It will also show how well you know the words in the spelling lists.

UNIT 20

Directions. Do the exercise in these steps:

Step 1. Go through the list and fill in the letters in the words that have blank letters.
Step 2. Go through the list again and write the *s* form of all the nouns and verbs that end in *y*.
Step 3. Find all the verbs that do not end in *y* and write their *ing* form. (This will include some of the words that had blank letters.)
Step 4. Find all the adverbs and after each one write *adv* on the line.
Step 5. Find all the pronouns and write *pron* on the line.
Step 6. For the words that remain, write the part of speech on the line. (You may use an abbreviation.)
Step 7. Answer the questions that follow the list.

1. n _ _ ce _____
2. difficulty _____
3. know _____
4. stop _____
5. organize _____
6. contain _____
7. enjoy _____
8. notice _____
9. th _ _ f _____
10. think _____
11. really _____
12. decide _____
13. often _____
14. rec _ _ ve _____
15. sincerely _____
16. company _____
17. produce _____
18. f _ _ ld _____
19. hit _____
20. earn _____
21. straight _____
22. deliver _____
23. bel _ _ ve _____
24. drop _____
25. recommend _____
26. again _____
27. th _ _ r _____
28. him _____
29. pharmacy _____
30. they _____
31. formerly _____
32. c _ _ ling _____
33. write _____
34. salary _____
35. come _____
36. immediately _____
37. require _____
38. n _ _ ghbor _____
39. recognize _____
40. valuable _____
41. sometimes _____
42. lose _____
43. always _____
44. w _ _ gh _____
45. she _____
46. apply _____
47. find _____
48. fr _ _ nd _____
49. type _____
50. Monday _____

Questions:

1. How many *ie* words are there? _____

2. How many *ei* words are there? _____

UNIT 20

3. How many nouns are there? _____
4. How many verbs are there? _____
5. How many adverbs are there? _____
6. How many pronouns are there? _____
7. How many other words are there? _____
8. What kind of words are the other words? _____

ANALYZING A PARAGRAPH

G. You have learned a great deal about the content and organization of paragraphs. Now read the following selection and decide whether it is a good paragraph.

    The custom of the wedding ring is more than a thousand years old. Its meaning goes back to the time when a man went out and kidnapped a girl for his bride. He tied her waist, wrists, and ankles with rope to show that she was his property. Throwing rice at a newly-wedded couple as they depart symbolizes the hope that they will be blessed with children. The idea of the wedding cake comes from ancient Rome, where the bride and groom shared an unleavened cake made of flour, salt, and water. This was thought to bring children and future happiness. Today the wedding cake has fancy decorations and much white frosting. Most wedding customs are very old, and they come from various lands. Throwing old shoes or tying them to the car of newlyweds derives from a custom of ancient Egypt. There the father of the bride handed her sandal to the groom, symbolizing a transfer of authority. Historians are not sure when or where the engagement ring began to enter the picture, but perhaps it began with the custom of giving a gift to the prospective bride. In the United States more than 90 per cent of the people become married.

1. What is the paragraph about?
2. Does it have a topic sentence?
3. Are the sentences in good order?
4. If you do not consider them in good order, how would you rearrange them?
5. Are any sentences irrelevant?
6. How is this paragraph developed?